BONDAGE
BUNGALOW
FANTASIES

BONDAGE BUNGALOW FANTASIES

Scripts for Canada's Most Famous Dominatrix

By Terri-Jean Bedford

iUniverse, Inc.

Bloomington

Bondage Bungalow Fantasies
Scripts for Canada's Most Famous Dominatrix

iUniverse books may be ordered through booksellers or by contacting:

iUniverse
1663 Liberty Drive
Bloomington, IN 47403
www.iuniverse.com
1-800-Authors (1-800-288-4677)

ISBN: 978-1-4759-6735-7 (sc)
ISBN: 978-1-4759-6736-4 (hc)
ISBN: 978-1-4759-6737-1 (ebk)

Library of Congress Control Number: 2012923556

Printed in the United States of America

iUniverse rev. date: 12/18/2012

CONTENTS

Dear Mistress,

I beg you to make me cry as much as possible.
Scold and humiliate me.
Use a wooden paddle, cane and a school strap.
Leave my hands red and my bottom well bruised.
Be nice to me when it's over.
Thank you Mistress.

(From a client letter)

PREFACE

I am Terri-Jean Bedford, Canada's most famous dominatrix. I have been in the news, often in the headlines, on and off for almost two decades. I have now written two books, this being the second.

In case you don't know about me, I ran two houses as a dominatrix. The first was from 1993 to 1994 just north of Toronto and it was closed by the police in a spectacular raid which led to a multi-year, multi-trial legal battle which was highly publicized. I opened a second house in downtown Toronto in 1998 and ran it until 2002. I had open houses to invite the press. So in addition to being a dominatrix I was a high profile activist. Naturally the nature of my trade and the issues arising in my trials made for great media. Finally, in 2010, Canada's prostitution laws were struck down and I was one of the three plaintiffs. The case is known as Bedford Versus Canada. During the interval between the victory over the laws and the subsequent first appeal by the Canadian Government, I published my first book.

That first book, *Dominatrix on Trial*, was my autobiography. I wrote about my life, legal battles and career as a dominatrix. The book has been optioned for the screen, and it seems that much of the fascination is with the clients. In that first book I also wrote about the scenes with the clients, about what kinds of men and women hired me, and even discussed why men wanted to be dressed as and pretend to be women or babies, put in bondage, tortured, humiliated or pretend to be school children. I am always being told "I wish you told more about these people", meaning both the clients and the doms.

I happened to have over three hundred pieces of correspondence from former clients or would-be clients. A word or two about that. I ran my so called "Bondage Bungalow" and later "Bondage Hotel and Millicent Farnsworth Sissy Maid Academy." In the Bungalow, which was pre-Internet, the clients would sometimes arrive with written scenarios, or mini scripts. Then they would fill out a questionnaire and sometimes write scripts then. Others would not write out scripts, but would rely on the questionnaire and leave the specifics to me. Clients of the Bondage Hotel would often send me their written scripts in advance via e-mail, which was by then widely used. I created a file for each correspondent or client from both facilities and placed the letters, as I will call them, along with their questionnaires, in those files. In my first book there was no space to share any of these with you, but there were so many interesting letters, some written with great care, that when I showed them to people I was told they were a virtual book in themselves. So, here we are. The letters make up Part 1 of this book.

In Part 2 of the book I depart from the letters, from the inner world of my clients, and tell you about my world, the world of the dom. I do so by describing in detail a couple of days from my life as a dominatrix. Then I share my answers to some interesting questions I've been asked over the years in a chapter called "Interesting Questions".

I want to emphasize that this book is about my clients and what it was like to be their dominatrix. That is why I say little in this book about my legal battles, or the issues surrounding them. Much is happening concerning all that as I write this book and prepare it for publication, but there is adequate coverage of those developments and what I have to say about them elsewhere.

I hope you enjoy, or at least find interesting, Bondage Bungalow Fantasies.

Terri-Jean Bedford
November 2012

INTRODUCTION

I am sharing over one hundred letters with you. I have over three hundred in my files.

The letters were usually not letters in the strict sense. My clients were asked to write out their main fantasy requests after they had been interviewed and had completed a questionnaire. In my second house, as I noted in the Preface, with the advent of the Internet, they would often send them to me before visiting.

The letters were often difficult to group or classify. There is usually much overlap. Fetishes are common to many letters, cross-dressing as well. Schoolroom fantasies also had elements of humiliation and torture. It goes on and on. So where there were overlapping themes I classed their fantasy letters based on themes emphasized.

The letters have been edited. Sometimes I, with the help of my editors, rewrote parts of them. If we didn't, you would have wished we did. Our concern is with their fantasies and thoughts. To have left the letters in their original form would have made for very difficult and unpleasant reading. That being said, we did not edit completely in the sense of a complete rewrite.

The first thing I edited out was what might be called administrative content: stuff like salutations, discussion of appointment dates and times, price enquiries and so forth. However, in Chapter 1 I left some of that in, to give you a sense of what was left out in later chapters. The next thing edited out was anything that could identify the writer. I changed names, locations, dates, ages, physical descriptions, references to family members and much more. Third, if something was poorly expressed we usually left it that way, only with corrected spelling, grammar and punctuation. That being said, the letters are all real. None were made up. If you doubt that, get in touch with me and I can show you some of them.

I found it necessary, in Chapter 2, to give the reader an understanding of the written materials and the Web sites the clients were referring to in their letters. I have included photographs of Web site pages and pamphlet covers and flyers and the like for this purpose as well.

You will also see several short letters, in Chapter 15, where they send simple thank you notes. I included them because I want to give you an impression of how grateful people were for the outlet.

I want to emphasize before going any further that we did not do everything they asked. We did not do any acts of "prostitution". That means that when they asked for, say, dildo insertions or to be masturbated, they were told this was not permitted. Neither, of course, was sexual intercourse of any description. At that time it was our understanding that you could whip someone for money but not massage their penis for money, even though prostitution was legal. Go figure. We did not cut, burn or leave permanent or even long lasting marks. We did not urinate or defecate on anyone. We did not strip for clients. We did not consent to any terrorist or kidnapping role play outside the facilities. We did not do these things for health and safety reasons, as well as because of possible legal ramifications. Nonetheless, these things were mentioned in their letters and I want you to see what was on their minds.

Almost none of the letters were from men who wanted women to play slaves to them, or anything like that. Requests like that were remarkably rare. There were women who wanted to be doms or dominate men, and I have a chapter of some of their letters. Almost all the men wanted to reverse the prevailing social role and be dominated by women.

My clients were a very diverse group. Sometimes this was indicated in the letters, but there was no guarantee that well written letters were from accomplished or successful people. Beyond that, you could never tell what the writer would be like in person. For example, some letters were short and poorly written, but the writer might look and speak like Laurence Olivier and judging by what they paid me, and sometimes paid to travel from abroad to see me, were highly successful or wealthy. So don't judge by what and how they write. Some very successful and distinguished men just don't express themselves well on paper. Others write well and do everything else poorly.

In reading the letters note how the writers talk about roles, props, equipment, costumes, and settings and how the dom should act. Note also, and this surprised me, they don't often convey what they want the dom to look like (aside from her attire). They rarely mention height, weight, bust size, skin color and so forth. What I found, however, is that they found larger women, both taller and heavier, more to their liking.

I want to offer some explanation here, and from time to time in the chapters which follow, of why these men went to such lengths to disclose their fantasies in writing, and the expense to act them out. I think you would want to know these things before reading their letters. So here are some things to keep in mind about why these guys do these things.

For one thing, it seems to me, now that I think of it, that you could consider these fantasies as excuses for the guy to merely look at the dom in costume, and look at her movements, as much as anything else. There was also the fact that she was paying detailed attention to him.

Also, men tend to suffer from low levels of self disclosure. They fear intimacy more than women, and reading the letters in this book you will understand why that is often the case. The mere act of disclosing a deep secret to a woman, or anyone, brings relief. Writing out a deep secret is easier for many than speaking it out. For one thing, you get to do a few drafts before letting it be seen, whereas when someone hears you speak it is the final draft, and it may not come out right. Some clients have told me that simply not having to keep "it" bottled up any more has been a life saver.

Then there is the relief that comes with acting out the fantasy. Let's say he starts with the thought of, say, a leather clad dominatrix with a whip tormenting him while he is helpless. Take it a step further, and you have films. A step further, and you have live shows. But the ultimate is when it is live, in private except for the participants, and you are the focus. The dream has come true, or almost true. She is not really a cruel woman torturer and you can stop the session any time, but you are very close. It is no longer just in the mind.

Then there is the fact that men who are not gay still usually have a feminine side in need of expression. Cross-dressing is the obvious example, sometimes combined with playing a sissy maid or feminized slave or schoolgirl. I had numerous American soldiers with combat experience, and even medals for bravery, who sought those fantasies.

I can't begin to tell you how many men have told me that the outlet my houses provided made them sane or saved their lives. I think they exaggerated a bit, but letting them act feminine or cry or feel helpless or see the woman of their dreams paying attention to them, seemed to have a major positive effect. I will never forget what one client said to me: "I was bored, lonely and anxious, and really had no reason to be. Then one of your mistresses whipped me while I was helpless and I cried uncontrollably. It had to have been thirty years or more since I had cried. For the next six months or more I was unexplainably happy and relaxed. People remarked that I looked and acted happier and healthier. All that after one good cry. People don't know how hard it is for a man to let himself cry."

Now that I have had my say in advance I ask that you not judge my clients. What *you* may find beautiful or arousing may make *others* laugh or think you are a sick pervert. You on the other hand, may be turned off by some of what you read. Ask yourself why in either case. Just don't judge. Some of the people whose fantasies you are going to read were or are your doctors, lawyers, judges, politicians, business leaders, clergymen, soldiers, friends, relatives, boyfriends, spouses or parents. You may even recognize yourself.

PART 1

The Letters

CHAPTER 1

I Need to See You

Much of my correspondence dealt with the simple logistics of directing the clients on how to get to my house, the fees and other things not related to their fantasies. Other correspondence was more explicit on why they were writing to me. Here is some of it in no particular order, so you get a sense of how initial correspondence would often come in.

* * *

Allow me to introduce myself. I am a submissive transvestite from The Netherlands and love to dress up and be used as a maid. I do have much experience but still need much training.

In The Netherlands the opportunities to get such training are very limited. Therefore I would love to spend my holiday (one or two weeks) abroad being trained to be a better maid. If you offer such opportunities, I would like to know.

Also, could you kindly inform me about the costs? Perhaps it would also be a nice opportunity to improve my English. Hoping to hear from you. Humble regards.

* * *

My fiancé and I are planning to be married on the fifth of June, and were curious about arranging part of our honeymoon to take place at your Bondage Hotel. We would like to make arrangements for Tuesday the seventh and perhaps the eighth as well. We are curious about what sort of access we would have to playrooms during an overnight visit, and what type of situations we could expect given the social club aspect of your establishment. In addition, we notice that you offer a weekend special. Is there by any chance a similar honeymoon special? Take care and thank you for your time.

*   *   *

This was addressed to one of my doms: the blond "glamazon", Contessa Cintra.

My name is Joe and I will be traveling to Toronto next week (May 13-17). I am a Christian and a virgin who has been struggling with lustful domination fantasies for a couple of months now. I know it is wrong and sinful but the temptation is sweetly delicious. I came upon your Web site. My fantasy is whether God can deliver me from the sinful desire of worshipping you. You are such a beautiful woman that I know it would be a great challenge to see if I could withstand the temptation of worshipping you. Thank you for your time.

*   *   *

As the date approaches I am becoming more and more anxious. I will arrive on Tuesday on United Airlines from Miami. Where should I go and how will we recognize each other?

I have been so far unsuccessful in obtaining either Canadian cash or a money order. I understand and respect the value of a deposit and have no problem with providing one. Given my failure (punishable?) to find it in Canadian form, might you grant an exception? I assume I will be able to exchange currency at the airport and will be prepared to pay the fee immediately.

Alternatively, I could send $300 in U.S. currency which you could bring to the airport and I could exchange it then. I am committed to being there, Madame, have a non refundable ticket and my "need" grows stronger as I fantasize. Barring disaster, I'll show—and appreciate your indulgence considering my discourtesy in making a problem of what should be simple.

On one page of the application I noted a suggestion that a letter of introduction be offered. I will prepare one with a brief general description, limits and interests. I expect more detail will be covered during some initial interview (under deliciously degrading conditions, I suppose and hope).

Again, thank you Madame. I greatly look forward to my three or more days with you and hope it will be an enjoyable encounter for you.

* * *

This is to introduce myself and to explain why I desire to be a student at your Academy. I am a retired government worker and recently became a widower. My wife passed away about two years ago.

I always had the desire to be dressed in ladies' clothing. This was suppressed during my marriage. Now recently being single again, I have been able to freely dress "en feminine". I am quite a novice in this area and desire to know more about my other self.

On my application you may note my variable selections from your workshop agenda. I would like to formally have a part of your curriculum made available to me. The feminine persona has always intrigued me and is quite a turn-on when dressed up. I have no "outside" experience and no makeup. Being advanced in age (sixty-six) I am intrigued as to how this can be done to transform me. I would desire to experience both areas and be part of your student faculty.

My schedule is quite flexible. Your consideration in this matter would be greatly appreciated.

* * *

Having seen your ad I knew I had to write to you. I love to cross-dress but I do need strict, no nonsense teaching on doing it properly! I also have a real love to really be sissified and be the taught young boy.

I was very thrilled and excited by your maturity, your big, solid capable size, especially your great, solid legs, and I loved your assistant. I picture you or a well off aunt who is saddled with raising a young nephew and you are assisted by a governess.

Your ad spoke of discipline and I hope this means corporal punishment, especially a prolonged bare bottom spanking while held helpless over your lap, or your assistant while you oversee as long as the end result is a severely reddened bum! Do you also offer correspondence training? I could send you photos of me dressed and my small size if you like. Please find enclosed $10 for your booklet.

* * *

I am a young submissive who would find it an honor to become the foot slave of such a beautiful goddess as you.

I would love to lick your high heels clean and then go on to give your hot and tired feet a refreshing tongue bath as well as lovingly sucking each toe. I have some experience at foot worshipping, but if you feel I am not up to your high standards you can trample me and crush my pathetic cock with your powerful feet.

If you feel I am worthy of your attention, please reply so I can arrange a time to worship you. In the meantime, may I be so bold as to ask for a picture of your perfect feet for me to worship before I get to kneel before the real thing. I hope to be your slave and footstool.

* * *

This client stressed what is crucial to most clients: that the dom convinces him that she enjoys the session.

I am serious and interested in booking a session. I am an experienced player, but have not played in a while. I am interested in one of your mistresses in particular (*he names her*), but before booking I would ask you to let me know the most appropriate person. I do not want someone who would dislike dominating me.

I love to be helpless, and at the hands of a strict dom. It is important to me that she at the very least be comfortable. I would love to be helpless, gagged, weights attached to me, then whipped and left there. When she returns I am tied and on the floor where she uses me as her foot slave, stepping on my face, making me lick her feet clean and so forth. I had better do a good job or I will receive more discipline. She rules, and can do what she wants (within limits). She can stand on me, sit on me and whip me. I am clean, sane, safe, respectful and obedient. I am also forty-nine years old, in good shape and health, six feet tall and 160 pounds.

* * *

Some clients asked about riding fantasies.

I am what you see: an older man, healthy, clean and sexually satisfied. I have always liked to play a submissive role to pretty girls or women starting from when my older sister and her girl friends would sit on me as a horse or wrestle me to the ground and sit on my chest and face when I teased or annoyed them (on purpose, knowing what would happen).

I always tried to create a situation with girls I dated whereby they would sit on me in various ways, often playing horse and cowboy. As a teenager I had an aunt and her friend who sat on me and rode me as a horse. We practiced and I became quite capable of moving (crawling) long distances and quickly for some time with them astride me.

I am intrigued by shapely legs, strong thighs and strong hips. The first question that comes to mind when I meet new women, or see them in articles or shows, is would I like her horse riding me and perhaps sitting on my face. I don't need sex or hand jobs. I will probably cum anyway. I hope using me as a horse or seat pleases my mistress and her governess, friend, associate or whatever. I have never been used by women over 140 pounds.

* * *

This letter was from a woman who saw my Web site and a documentary report about my house on television.

Wow, your new place looks amazing. Hope to maybe get a chance to check it out and maybe spend a night. I'm all excited about the potential available. Do you rent out to small groups or just couples? I'm trying to plan a surprise scene for someone's birthday. If you do, is it still the same price for use of the dungeon?

* * *

My fiancé and I are hoping to travel to Toronto for our honeymoon a few days after our wedding on July 15. We would like to know if you have any nights available a few days after that. We'd also like any and all information you can give us on accommodations, services, prices and so forth. We are looking for a mostly private getaway room with all the fun toys to play with. We got a general idea from the Web site, but would like to have more details about what is at your hotel. One last thing, how far are you located from Queen Street West? We are traveling from Ohio in the United States and are not familiar with the area. Also, we'd like to know how the charges appear on our credit card statements, as it will be possibly paid for by one of our relatives, and we like to keep this sort of thing to ourselves.

*   *   *

I spoke to you briefly this morning. However, I felt uncomfortable so I told you that I will call later. However writing this seems much easier. I called you because I need your help to become a better man. After what I experienced over the weekend, I realize that women are the superior gender and men are just pigs. On Saturday, my sister and some of her friends caught me trying to stimulate myself with a ham and cheese sandwich. On Sunday, I was caught naked, again trying to stimulate myself by putting my penis through a small hole in a steel fence.

I really want to change my ways and start pleasing women instead of myself. I would do it by myself, however being a man I am weak, stupid, and lack the mental focus to accomplish such a task. I know I sound hopeless and such a loser and don't blame you if you reject my plea. If you change your mind you can e-mail me or better still, call me at (*he gave his number*) between four and five on weekdays.

*   *   *

I am a thirty-five year old white male, look twenty-five, am five feet eight inches tall and weigh 180 pounds. It has always been my fantasy to be a girl. I started cross-dressing in third grade. I would love to attend your academy this year and become a sissy maid for life. I am willing to do what it takes to become a sissy girl. I can clean house really well.

*   *   *

I am interested in your services. I have no cross-dressing or submissive experience at all. It is my desire to be dressed up like a girl. Can you please explain the difference in what you offer? Your great Web site mentioned petticoat punishment and sissy maid. It has always been my fantasy to be dressed up like a girl figure skater, in those lovely dresses, but after reading your Web site I feel I may be a sissy maid.

I am just looking into these desires that I have. How do I know if I am really submissive or just want to be dressed like a girl? I am a twenty-three year old single guy who can afford some sessions. Is it uncommon for younger men to have these desires?

*   *   *

Thank you for your thoughtful note and permission to speak. My e-mail of yesterday referred to a series of questions related to a proposed plan to come to Toronto at the end of May. To save you time, I am copying the note at the bottom of this message. I need to book flights well in advance, so I hope you understand the urgency, despite the fact it is nearly six weeks away.

Given the fact that your program in your latest note is different from that requested in my note, I will obviously have to adjust, but hope that we can agree on the dates, as I am picking a period when my vanilla wife will be traveling.

I am very apprehensive about and also fearful about this venture, especially about your out of class expedition, partly because of my novice status and my age—very humiliating. But it goes without saying that my mistress is very pleased with your plans for me. I'm sorry for being so outspoken.

(*Here is the earlier note he referred to. He had been writing to one of my staff*).

Dear Headmistress. My mistress let me read the very detailed information on your Web site, and I see now that I have broken your rules. My humble apologies and I beg that doesn't disqualify me from attending classes! Mistress and I are thinking that I should arrive in Toronto on a Thursday morning and then fly back to Boston either Saturday or Sunday. Please advise whether this will provide enough time to address the following segments: personal preparation, personal hygiene, lady's maid training and dressing and preparation.

* * *

This man asked for an Asian dom I had with me. Around the year 2000 the kind of services I offered were mainly sought by occidentals or their descendents, but things were beginning to change. I had much editing to do here as his English was very broken. I trust I left some sense of that.

My name is [*he gave his very Asian sounding name*]. I viewed your Web page and it's excellent and I think it's the best S&M site in Canada. I visit Toronto from time to time and sure will make an appointment for a session with Chinese Mistress or others. My fantasy is to have a female play an executioner whose job it is to execute me. I also love forced bondage, where I just pretend to resist. I am to be pinned down, tied up and dragged. Then the executioner in a provocative uniform comes in equipped with instruments of punishment such as a billy stick, handcuffs and a dagger. My fetish is to be frightened by her and for her to punish me in advance of my supposed impending execution. Please reply if Mistress China Doll is into this fetish and role play.

* * *

I know I have no business talking with you, but do you do e-mail training? If so please inform me on how to go about getting started. I would love to serve you in any way I can. Thank you for your time.

I told him in reply that for the price of an actual session, he could have the time via e-mail, with a minimum charge, paid in advance. He did not follow up.

* * *

I saw your interview on television on Monday, and I thought you were wonderful. I really respect what you're doing (*he was referring to my legal battle at that time*), and I hope you continue to provide this valuable service for a long time to come. I am personally interested in obtaining your services, because I have a great fetish for female domination. My only concern is whether you cater to males who are twenty-seven years old. Hopefully this isn't a problem. I think you are very sexy, and I would like some information on how I can arrange an appointment with you sometime. I do hope to hear from you really soon and look forward to your patronage.

* * *

I live in Georgia and travel to Toronto several times a year on business. I have been a closet submissive most of my life. I'm fifty-five and have had long term relationships with several female doms. I would like to come to your place in Toronto next Friday at five o'clock and stay until noon Tuesday. Once we have discussed the rules and so forth I will give you my payment. Please see that I am committed and not permitted to leave until Tuesday morning, under any conditions.

I am experienced in heavy spanking, whipping, medium caning and medium and heavy cock and ball torture. However I cannot get an erection because my prostate gland has been removed. I have experienced long periods of bondage, electro torture, foot worship, fart smelling, being a piece of human furniture and an ashtray, face sitting, and the list goes on. I am claustrophobic and get faint during suspension. I appreciate true dominants, not just actresses. Let me know if you need further information.

* * *

Mom finally passed away, so I have been down in New Jersey and not available these past six weeks. I am now back in the community, but I can't tell you how much her death has really affected me. Though I am still on sabbatical I am currently overseeing a small community project. Since mom passed a lot of my thinking has turned towards thoughts of dressing and becoming her. I know it sounds a little weird, but it seems more and more of my thoughts are turning towards the feminine. I'm leaning more and more to leaving here soon, and as I have expressed to you before would like to explore what it might be like to become this woman that I think I might be. Thanks for all your patience and please help me through this transition in my life.

*   *   *

I am a Danish transvestite (still in the closet) with a leaning for being submissive. I have seen your Web site regard your maid academy and it seems a perfect place for me in order to be forced into my role as a submissive transvestite and maid, where I can be kept away from my manhood and kept firmly under control. But also a place where I could learn maid's skills and skills that would help me pamper a mistress. It sounds too good to be true. Could you please inform me as to prices, how long a stay you would recommend and what times it is possible to visit. As I understand it you provide full boarding.

*   *   *

I have a question about your training. I am a forty-four year old male, who cross-dresses in a maid's outfit and provides services for my wife. I would like to attend your training some day, but I need to know if you are willing to train someone in a wheelchair. I am a paraplegic with full use of my upper body, but cannot walk or stand. Please let me know.

*   *   *

I understand the training program has been finalized to begin Wednesday evening and end Sunday afternoon. I plan to arrive in Toronto from Philadelphia and proceed to your Academy for registration.

There are several requests that I am making for your gracious consideration. I am in my fifties and am diabetic (controlled) so must bring and take medication. Second, as my wife is not is not aware of where I will be, it will be necessary for me to make and receive two, maybe three phone calls during the four days to ensure all is well on both sides. I will bring my cell phone, which can accept voice mail messages.

Please also advise whether an information letter is required from me in addition to the foregoing e-mails and this note. If so, what additional information is required?

If all is in order, please advise me if you need a deposit and in what amount so I can arrange for an international money order to be sent to you. When flights have been finalized I will provide you with more complete information.

*   *   *

I wonder if you would mind if I ask a few questions about coming for extended stays. I assume that in the evenings there will be homework to do. Is it possible that on occasion in the evening or on the weekend other activities may be scheduled by the headmistress, such as rope bondage, interrogations, trips out for humiliating experience and sensory deprivation? Should I assume that there is normally a school uniform? Would it be possible to wear other outfits such as hooker clothes, baby outfits, sexy underwear, understanding of course that this in itself may be the subject of punishment? At night I like to wear diapers, plastic pants, and baby clothes and be bound in my crib. Would that also be possible? As I would have to fly to Toronto for school, would it be possible to be met at the airport and brought to the school? If I arrived on a weekend, would it be possible to start my education stay with an interrogation, some torture and bondage to get me to confess my transgressions such that school is then part of my re-education? I would very much appreciate any guidance you can give me.

*   *   *

Up until about two years ago I was dressing up behind closed doors. It was then that I thought it was time I told my wife. At the time I thought it was a good time to tell her because we were into a little bondage and discipline, where she was my mistress. When I brought it out into the open about me dressing as a woman it was like a ton of bricks hit the room. It didn't go over too well because she gets ticked off when she sees me putting on women's clothes. So now we have our separate rooms. Do I have to go back behind closed doors? I keep telling her she needs a maid to look after her needs. All I get is that look of steel. I did tell her that I was going to enroll in your academy for sissy maids. Her answer was to say "so what?" I still think if I was to graduate from your academy there might still be some light at the end of the tunnel for her to accept my other side.

P.S: Dressing up goes way back to when I was a teenager. I would take my sister's clothes and put them on. Back then I wished I was born a girl instead of a boy. I am fifty-four years old now. Maybe you could help me break the ice with my wife.

*　*　*

I am a middle aged company executive and have been good and evil at alternate times. Later in the month I may spend a few days in Toronto and would like to take this opportunity to find out the truth about myself with the assistance of a philosopher. A friend has heard about you and advises me to write to enquire. I like to control but on the other hand enjoy serving attractive ladies. Do you think that I am unusual for having these strange feelings? Do you think I should come to see you, and if yes what would you be prepared to teach me and what is the tribute? Also, how can I locate you aside from the e-mail address? My friend has not provided other information in respect of your services and means of contact. Thank you in anticipation of any advice given.

*　*　*

The September 2001 terrorist attacks reduced my visitors from outside Canada, and indeed within it. This letter, an e-mail, was dated October 2, 2001.

I am so sorry not to have gotten in touch with you sooner. Since the eleventh of September my world has been spinning. A sister-in-law of mine has gone missing in New York due to the attack at the WTC and my priorities have changed 180 degrees since then. I've been to NYC for a week trying to help with my brother's family while they are caught up in this terrible situation. You may imagine that most other things in my life are almost forgotten. I was supposed to spend the month of October with you folks and as you can see I didn't make it. I am so sorry. I will write again.

*　*　*

This letter, an e-mail, was also dated October 2, 2001. The Internet was interrupted by the security concerns after the September attacks. This client was employed in computer security in the Toronto area.

It is great to see your Web page back up and it is looking great! Baby Angie and I (as well as a few other age players) intend to sell some toys at an AIDS benefit in November. We would very much like to hand out your advertisements during this event. We have been very busy with the mundane world (Yuk) and have not had time to visit anywhere. In addition the latest political events have been a rather big downer and source of depression.

When you have a moment (we understand you are busy) let me know what items have sold from the things I left there so I don't have to make them all over for the benefit. In addition if you have any items you want to have sold for you then by all means let us know. We were curious when you had planned to have another baby party. We have met some new Toronto friends and they want to come with us (nervous types) to meet you and see your facilities. We imagine you plan some type of Halloween event and would love to know what your plans are. I have my edit program working and would be delighted to take some photos for your Website (or advertisements) if you wish.

We are really looking forward to some free time in the near future and would love to stay over. Because of fears of net terrorism Baby Angie is working overtime adding security systems at work and it is really a pain on our social life!

We hope to see you soon and all our best to the crowd.

*　　*　　*

I have reviewed your Web site and would like to enquire about your enrolment procedures. I know I am expected to provide you with a letter of introduction and personal preferences so I beg your indulgence and request that you review my history. I only hope you will find me acceptable for enrolment.

I truly believe in female superiority. I have had many forced feminization experiences but still consider myself a novice in this area. My goal is to become a full time live-in maid/servant/lover/companion to a dominant (genetic) woman and live full time (or as much as possible) as a woman myself. I believe in complete forced feminization with strict discipline. My interests also include strict bondage and discipline training for both my mistress's pleasure and any necessary behavior modification I may require. I love all things feminine (makeup, high heels, lingerie, stocking, garters, bras, panties, dresses, skirts, maid uniforms, gowns, jewellery and so forth). I am in my mid forties, so a mistress between forty and fifty would be ideal (after proper education, of course).

I have reviewed your course offerings and there is so much to choose from, so many fabulous choices. Since I am not sure whether I should be enrolled in your slave school or your sissy maid academy, I will leave it to you to determine what is best for me, as it should be. Again, even though I have had some experience in forced feminization and serving dominant women, I still consider myself a novice. So there it is. I only hope you find this enquiry acceptable and will deem it worthy of a response. Thank you so very much my dearest Headmistress for even bothering to read this letter.

MADAME'S HOUSE

CANADA'S FINEST BONDAGE HOTEL

BED & BREAKFAST FOR FETISHISTS

Elegant Victorian Hospitality

Some of my advertising

Madame de Sade's
Bondage Hotel
Sanctum Sanctorium

A Private Dungeon Oasis
Four Poster Double King Size
Bondage Bed
Complete with all the trimmings
Breakfast in Bed
Private Bath
Immaculate Facilities
Wake-up Calls
Kitchen
Laundry Service
Maid Service
Professional Services
by Doms' & Subs (no sex)
Private Parking
All Major Credit Cards Accepted
By Reservation Only

Madame de Sade's
House of Fetish and Dungeons

An Adult Theme Park Getaway
&
Role-Play Facility

Four Floors of Fun
Classical Victorian Settings
Library
Classroom
Kitchen
Parlor
Adult Baby Nursery
Sensory Deprivation Dungeon
Medieval Dungeon
Sissy Maid Academy & Charm
School
Open Daily * Noon till Midnight

Madame's Vintage Boutique
*Consignment * Buy * Sell * Trade*
*Open Daily * Noon till 7:00 pm*

The
Millicent Farnsworth
Sissy Maid Academy
& Charm School

For
Crossdressers and Gentlemen
n need of Behavior Modification
through
Forced Petticoat Training
and Corporal Punishment

Learn to
Walk, Talk and Act
Like a Real Lady
Whether you like it or not!

The Faculty
Madame de Sade ~ Headmistress
Contessa Cintra ~ Vice Principal
Lady Marquette ~ Instructor
Lotus ~ Instructor

Complete Transformation Makeovers
Extensive Wardrobes
Body Shaves

Adult Baby Nursery

Oh, show me pray
the pathway back.
The Pathway that leads
to Childhood Land.
Oh why did I in search for gain
abandon Mother's Guiding Hand.
Oh how I crave but to retire,
and not be roused by vain desire.
To shut my weary tired eyes
To Be A Child Again

Complete Nursery
Giant Adult Baby Crib
Play Pen * High Chairs
Diapers (disposable and cloth)
Regular Diaper Change and Feedings
Jumpers * Nighties * Dresses
Toys & Games
Playtime * Bedtime Stories
Baby Bondage and Discipline

Cast of Characters
Mommy Dearest ~ Madame de sade
Aunties * Sisters * Babysitters
Authentic Family Environment

Rates

Bondage Hotel
$150.00 single
$250.00 couple
Weekend
$300.00 single
$400.00 couple

Dungeon Rental
$75.00 1hr
Tour and Consultation
$50.00 1/2 hr
**All patrons must attend a general
consultation before engaging in S/M activities**
Spanking Special
$60.00 novice
$80.00 advanced
$125.00 cane or paddling

Sissy Maid Academy
Full Day $500.00
Half Day $350.00
Full Day & Overnight $650.00
Sissy Camp - 3 days and 2 nights
$1200.00

House of Fetish and Dungeons
Bondage and Discipline
**Rates will vary depending upon the nature of
request.
Novice $200.00 Advanced $300.00 per hour
Monthly House Party Ticket $60.00**

Madame de Sade's

BONDAGE HOTEL

SWINBOURNE

TV Schedule: Noon till 2pm

Free Interactive Variety Talk Show with
Canada's Most Notorious Dominatrix
and her Beautiful Mistresses, Kinky Friends,
Sissy Maids, Famous Drag Queens,
Adult babies, and other unusual guests.

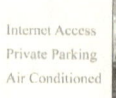

The dorm

The office of the Headmistress

Two former soldiers march for their mistress

School time for sissies

My daughter Janet punishing a slave and getting her feet kissed

The much loved and feared Contessa Cintra

CHAPTER 2

Here is My Application

Clients found out about me when they saw an ad. When I ran my house in Thornhill the ads were in the trade papers, such as fetish or entertainment magazines. For my last house there was also the Internet. I have put some samples of the images they saw when they went to my Web site ahead of this chapter to give you an idea of what they are referring to in the letters.

My Thornhill house from 1993 to 1994 was before the Internet, so they called and made an appointment. I asked them to write up a detailed role play scenario, or more than one, if they wished to bring it with them. When they arrived they filled out a questionnaire, were interviewed and would give me their written scenario. They could also take a few minutes and write one there, if the interview was not detailed enough. Usually it was, and I would often help them construct it. It is so difficult for so many men to disclose their inner desires. Then they would have a tour and possibly stay for a session or more often make an appointment.

When I ran my Toronto house from 1998 to 2002, more and more clients had use of the Internet. I often got letters of enquiry in response to them seeing my Web site, and sometimes in response to ads I placed. In these initial contacts they gave me fantasy and background details right off the bat. What we (I had others helping me eventually) did was e-mail the questionnaire, and tell them the cost for a tour and initial appointment. So I now had four ways to get the information I needed: initial e-mail, questionnaire, fantasy request letter after the initial e-mail and the interview.

The Questionnaire

After the client, almost always a man, listed basic information such as name, phone number, e-mail address, height, weight and so forth he would answer yes or no to whether any of a number of listed health or medical conditions existed. While he was doing this the mistress conducting the interview would observe his movements, reflexes, breathing, flexibility, body fat and anything else that caught her attention. She would write down her observations in the file.

Some of the more important health or medical questions were: whether he had an HIV test (and the results if he did), whether he ever had any sexually transmitted disease, if he had ever seen a psychiatrist, whether he was wearing contact lenses and whether he was currently on any medication or made regular use of any mind altering substance or if he was receiving any other treatments aside from counseling or medication, such as chiropractic.

Then, to be thorough, he would circle or check any health issues listed if they applied to him. Here is how the list of seventy-five items began and ended: acne, allergies, arthritis, angina, asthma, athlete's foot, backache, and bad breath, bed-wetting . . . . warts, ulcers, tendonitis.

Then he would circle or check off items from a long list, which were listed on the questionnaire as "Techniques". These included fetish objects or certain desires such as bondage and so forth. I am now giving you the list of all items on the questionnaire, but I am presenting it differently. I rearranged the order and manner in which it is presented to make for easier reading. And yet again, I emphasize, that this is just given to find out their predilections. Our services did not include all that was listed. But knowing in detail what interested the clients did allow us to suggest alternatives that were acceptable, which he may not have considered. In no particular order, here is the list:

- Bondage and Being Ignored:
  in view of others
  in isolation
  gagged
  blindfolded
  with earplugs

- Sensory Deprivation:
  locked coffin
  with further restraint
  via non-removable hood or mask

- Being Massaged:
  being tortured by a masseuse while in restraints
  being tortured by a masseuse while not in restraints

- Massaging a Mistress:
  while cross-dressed
  while hooded or blindfolded
  while supervised and punished by another mistress

- Forced Enemas:
  while in restraint
  while not in restraint

- Cross-dressing:
  for purposes of display to others (give preferences)
  as punishment
  as part of a classroom scenario
  to be taken out in public to "pass"
  just to feel immobilized

- Spanking:
  by hand
  with an implement (specify implement)

- Whipping with a:
  light whip
  cat-o-nine tails
  bull whip
  rubber whip
  snakeskin whip
  leather whip
  paddle
  cane

        bamboo pole
        bundled switches
        chains
        belt
        riding crop
        other (specify)

- Interrogation Scenes:
  provide details

- Worship:
  body
  bare feet
  feet in boots
  general
  by kissing
  by groveling
  verbally

- Servitude:
  give details

- Golden or Brown Showers:
  being urinated on or defecated on

- Cutting:
  being cut for real
  being threatened with cutting
  specify where cutting to be done
  specify instruments to be used

- Suffocation via:
  drowning
  pillow
  mask
  hands
  other means (specify)

- Mummification using:
  bandages
  regular sheets
  leather sheets
  a sack
  a leather bag
  other (specify)

- Bondage preferences:
  rope
  twine
  cotton
  wire
  leather straps
  chains
  nylon stockings
  handcuffs
  steel shackles
  rubber tubing
  straight jacket
  harness
  other (specify)

- Burning with:
  candle wax
  a cigarette
  a branding iron
  a lighter
  a torch
  other (specify)

- Gagging using:
  rubber ball in mouth
  adhesive tape
  dildo
  stockings
  the heel of a woman's shoe
  a heavy mask
  other (specify)

- Electric Shocks:
  specify where
  specify accompanying restraint

- Tickling with:
  fingers
  feathers
  vibrators
  other implements (specify)

- Imprisonment in a:
  cage
  cell
  closet
  box
  trunk
  coffin
  barrel
  crate
  other (specify)

- Suspension:
  by the hands using chains
  in the bondage swing
  other (specify)

- Wrestling with a Mistress or Mistresses:
  while partially restrained (specify)
  while blindfolded
  while blindfolded and partially restrained
  while blindfolded and deafened
  while not restrained
  in mud
  in water
  specify number of mistresses
  specify limits

- Infantilism:
  being bathed, powdered and diapered
  being put into baby clothes and a playpen or crib
  being bottle fed
  being tickled and cuddled
  other (specify)

- Being Stomped On:
  by a mistress in bare feet
  by a mistress in high heels
  by a mistress in boots
  while restrained (specify restraint)
  while not restrained
  other (specify)

- Having Your Hair Pulled:
  while in restraint (specify)
  while not restrained
  specify which hair (scalp, eyebrows, eyelids, body, pubic or head)
  specify limits

- Fetish Items You Generally Like Worn by a Mistress:
  glasses
  sun glasses
  Mir caps
  nurse uniforms
  doctor coats
  business suits
  high leather boots
  regular leather boots
  stiletto heels
  girdles
  corsets
  garters and nylons
  pantyhose
  rubber cat suits
  leather cat suits
  clear vinyl sheets with little on underneath

    leather gloves
    rubber gloves
    long painted nails
    shaved head
    short hair
    long hair
    blond hair
    red hair
    black hair
    brown hair
    grey hair
    white hair

- Mistress Types:
  tall
  short
  fat
  medium build
  skinny
  muscular
  thick thighs
  Asian
  Black
  White
  with an accent (specify)
  perfumed
  smelling of body odor

As I had mentioned before, the mistress would take notes during the interview or while the client filled out the questionnaire. By the time the client had seen our Web site and answered the questionnaire he had more ideas in his mind before communicating a fantasy or fantasies in his interview or at the end of the questionnaire. You can see above that not every possibility occurs to someone on the spot. All this helped us to give him his money's worth, and of course encourage additional and repeat business.

The Millicent Farnsworth Sissy Maid Academy

In my Toronto house, part of the offering was the Millicent Farnsworth Sissy Maid Academy and Charm School, which basically focused on cross-dressing combined with slave training. So if they read the Web site and said their interest was that, as opposed to the dungeon or slave activity without cross-dressing and so forth we gave them a different questionnaire. The Academy questionnaire did not have to be as detailed as the other one, because we already knew the direction of interest. Here are some of the typical questions that would appear after the basic information on contact numbers, how they heard about us, physical condition and so forth has been given.

- What is your previous cross-dressing experience?
- Do you go out in public cross-dressed?
- Do you find public outings a pleasant experience?
- How would you describe your best female persona?
- What is your favorite female look?
- Are you married? Provide details.
- What do you think will be the difficult areas for you as a Sissy Maid?
- A Sissy Socialite is refined, with poise and good manners. Do you prefer directing your schooling to this area?
- How else can Millicent Farnsworth help you?
- Please attach a letter outlining the session or scenario for your time with us if you have not already done so above.

* * *

So now you see how I came to possess such as large collection of letters or letter-like write-ups that outlined role-play scenarios. Let's now have a look at some of those scenarios.

CHAPTER 3

Take Me to School

This classroom fantasy was quite common. I had classrooms in both my houses. Classroom fantasies were among the most elaborate.

*   *   *

I was thinking about visiting from May 22 to May 24. I will tell you what I have in mind for this fantasy. Let me start with this detailed description of the fantasy I need to fulfill.

I would like to be treated as a five year old schoolboy in uniform (I hope you have a schoolboy uniform that I can use) at a nineteen fifties traditional English school with discipline, punishment and scolding. I would like to have my entire body shaved with the exception of my head and legs. I would like to be put in a classroom for eight hours a day to do actual school work such as math, English and science, complete with homework assignments. If at all possible I would like to have a different teacher every day, dressed in a professional manner like a real school teacher would be. If possible it would be great to have other students in the class, especially girls (I have never seen a girl spanked before). When it comes to spanking I've only experienced hand spankings. I am willing to take mild to severe spanking over the pants and perhaps on the bare bottom too. I've never experienced any implements before and would also be open to that. I've never experienced the cane and perhaps I would like to feel it over the pants.

One thing I would like to experience is to be sent to the Headmistress's office for punishment because I was just too bad for the teacher to handle. I would like to be watched at all times by the teacher, even in the bathroom, with the exception of free time. I would like to have a timetable made up outlining every hour of the day in terms of where I will be and what I will be doing. At bed time I would like to be tucked into bed with a very sore and red bottom every night and put into a diaper too. In the morning I prefer to be woken and given a bath and spanked to start the day.

This is my fantasy. Can you please help me fulfill it? Your domain is highly recommended for this type of scene. If you can do this are meals included? I've seen a picture of you madam, but may I also have descriptions of the other teachers who will be involved?

Now a description of me in real life [*he gives it*]. I'm employed, honest, have a good sense of humor and am intelligent. I realize I am asking a whole lot, but I have to fulfill this fantasy before I get married. I'm not rich by any means but I do work and I've been saving to fulfill this fantasy, so please keep this in mind when you give me the price. Last but not least, the only thing I expect is that you be totally honest with me.

* * *

Miss Guinevere was one of my staff at the so-called Bondage Bungalow from 1993 to 1994. She was at that time about forty years of age. Many men preferred older doms. When they were school children their female teachers appeared old to them. I was also referred to as Mistress Marie, usually for scenarios involving a Headmistress, or school principal, in which the doms might use me as a threat for the clients. For example, they might say," If you continue to cry out I'll have to tell the Headmistress". Thus, the dom, or female teacher, had power over the little boy, while the Headmistress had power over the teacher.

Andy is a student in Miss Guinevere's high school English class. She starts class by announcing she has purchased a new strap. She has previously warned students about not doing their homework. She is playing with the strap in her hands. She asks if anyone has not done their homework. Andy says he has not. He is told to stand in the corner and think about being strapped. She continues to teach the class. Then she says: "O.K. Andy, come and get it." She gives him 3 hard strokes on each hand. Then she sits Andy down and gives him an assignment, a writing assignment, stating that she will correct it when finished. While Andy is working, she looks over his shoulder and so forth, brushing past and around him, occasionally up against him. She warns him that the strap will be used again if a good job is not done.

When he is finished she corrects the work, finding mistakes and sloppiness. She straps Andy three times on each hand and tells him she knows he can do better. Andy must stand in the corner while Miss Guinevere goes for a discussion with the principal, Mistress Marie.

A few minutes later Miss Guinevere returns. She says: "I've got bad news Andy. Mistress Marie is fed up with the attitudes of the students and she wants to make an example of you. You are to accompany me to her office." Miss Guinevere takes Andy by the hand up to Mistress Marie's office.

Mistress Marie, assisted by Miss Guinevere, puts Andy into light bondage, hands tied up, to receive a thrashing as an example. Mistress Marie says she will show Miss Guinevere how to treat unruly students. She gives Andy three hard strokes with each of her implements, and instructs Miss Guinevere to do the same. This is to show me the range of her implements. They each use a paddle. They each use a cat-o-nine tails whip. They each use a strap. You can ad-lib from there.

*   *   *

Here a male client wishes to pretend he is a schoolgirl.

Amanda enters the room of the Mistress of Discipline and hands over a behavior report given by Amanda's teacher. Mistress studies the report and gives a brief lecture. Mistress indicates she will have to give Amanda much stronger discipline since this is Amanda's second visit to her. Mistress then orders Amanda to stand or kneel in the corner, facing the wall, and reflect on her conduct.

Some minutes later, Mistress summons Amanda to approach her desk. Mistress informs Amanda she is to receive a number of punishments for her various misdeeds. Mistress also makes special mention of a good ass caning as well as a disciplinary enema.

Mistress rises, picks up a ruler and orders Amanda to hold out her left hand. Mistress gives further instructions about extending the arm well out and straight with palm fully open. Mistress grasps Amanda's wrist, taps the ruler on Amanda's palm, then administers good, sharp strokes to the middle of the palm (about ten strokes). The process is repeated for the right hand.

Mistress positions a straight back chair in the middle of the room. With ruler paddle in hand, she sits down and orders Amanda to stand at Mistress's right side. Amanda is ordered to lift her skirt and slip and lie over Mistress's lap. Mistress takes some time making sure Amanda is properly positioned so her bottom is well up. Mistress then tugs Amanda's panties well inside the crease. A sharp, sound spanking follows (twenty or more strokes). Extras may be given if Amanda does not stay quite still. At the conclusion Amanda is told to stand up and fix her clothing.

Amanda is then ordered to stand in the middle of the room. Mistress picks up a cane, flexes it, swishes it, then mentions some serious misdeeds for which Amanda is about to be caned. Multiple canings and strapping follow.

Some suggested positions are as follows: bending over grasping ankles, feet slightly apart, knees braced back; same, but with skirt and slip raised, and caning over panties; standing facing the wall (four feet away), palms flat against the wall, skirt and slip raised, panties lowered, cane and strap used; kneeling on a low stool or on the seat of a chair, panties bent well inside the crease so the cheeks are bare, cane and strap used; bending over a desk, bench or stool, clothes raised, panties pulled up inside the crease, possibly with various implements used; caning or strapping with hand/leg cuffs—bending over a bench, table or desk or hung upright from the ceiling.

An enema is then administered. It should be quite warm (not hot) using plain water or a mild soap solution. Amanda lies on a table or bench on her left side with her knees drawn up. The nozzle is to be inserted gently and carefully. The flow is to be shut off from time to time to allow Amanda to adjust to the discomfort level. At the conclusion Mistress orders Amanda to bend over for some strokes of the cane before being permitted to visit the toilet.

After discipline Amanda returns from the toilet wearing a sling. She is then ordered to bend over a desk, table or stool. Mistress inserts a well lubricated butt plug, adjusts the sling and then administers a final caning and strapping. Please note that accuracy of placement is crucial, meaning the mid-section of the buttocks. The cane should not strike the tailbone or hips. The tip of the cane should not reach beyond the mid-section of the right cheek. Impact should be over both cheeks; hence position of

Mistress and angle of delivery is important. Strokes should be given in fifteen to twenty second intervals. Keeping Amanda in suspense is as important as the infliction itself. The number of strokes should not be less than ten. Intensity of delivery should increase gradually. Mistress should be able to gauge from Amanda's reactions what intensity is appropriate during Amanda's caning. Mistress should caution Amanda to remain still and silent. Additional strokes might be given if Amanda is not very cooperative.

Note as well the positioning of Mistress for discipline. Some moments should be given to careful and precise positioning prior to any discipline. Mistress might also manually help get Amanda to properly adopt a particular position. These preliminaries do enhance the acute sense of nervous anticipation of what is about to happen.

He had his session and then another. Here is what he wrote to me some days later. Of course I had to tell him that to fully create his fantasy would be very expensive, if even possible, but we were able to do much of what he asked. Note how he now drifts away from the classroom aspect.

I think we have made good progress in exploring the shadow side of my personality, namely the feminine. I definitely feel more comfortable with this aspect of myself. Acting out my fantasies under your direction has been both liberating and fulfilling. The truth makes us free even if it is on the dark side of our personality. Thanks for your strong and creative directions and supervision.

During the third session perhaps we can develop the "young lady" dimension of my being a female. To date I have found the following procedures particularly helpful.

Standing before you naked in my birthday suit I feel very vulnerable, passive, at your disposal, ready to be molded according to your female design. I feel submissive, feminine, your pet student or your darling daughter. Perhaps you could extend this scene and make this feminine experience deeper and more pervasive of my personality. I count on your creative imagination to devise suitable methods.

Being ordered to put on panties or even more significantly having panties put on one is a very unique experience. Panties are a clear sign of the female. They are designed for the pussy, not the cock. Wearing them is a clear expression of one's femininity. Having to stand, parade or model one's panties in public not only expresses one's femininity, but actually goes some way in creating the girl or young lady. It is an effective form of castration leaving only the appearance of a pussy. Perhaps you might find a way of highlighting this event too. The other clothing items such as the bra, stockings, dress, etc. are significant in supporting and confirming the meaning of the panties.

I would find you playing with me as your pet student or dear daughter particularly helpful in exploring and developing my feminine dimension. This could take different forms. You could tease me about being dressed that way and about being made to act and even to some extent be a young lady. You could embarrass me in front of my friends (both girls and boys) by having me display my panties or allow them to explore various aspects of my body. You could use your wonderful hands to explore and posses every part of me and thus help me to fully experience, accept and even embrace my femininity. You could have me sit on your knee and have me tell you why I like being a girl, what particular clothes I'd like to wear and so forth. I am sure your imagination could devise many ways for me to experience my femininity in a playful, gentle but firm way.

Some discipline is probably in order. Light spankings across your knee are most appropriate, with a good deal of tickling. Finally, something should be said about relating to boys as a young lady. In some ways boys define girls and so I should be expected to relate, submit, and even encourage the attention and affection of boys. I am sure you have ways of bringing this experience about.

I feel that now that the hard spankings and the school model are less effective in attaining our goal.

*   *   *

What follows are lengthy excerpts from two long letters from a man who lived about four hours from Toronto. He saw me on television while one of my appeals was in progress and his references to my fight and so forth relate to that. Like so many, he did not have the financial resources to realize his dreams more than occasionally. His letters were long and hand written. I have edited the writing quite a bit, and here I only give you about half of what he sent me. I actually did have him in to my house a few times before I closed and I tried to accommodate him. When I closed I lost contact with him because I told him I was sick and he respected that and said he would not be a burden on me. He was shy and polite.

Can you imagine how much stress it would have been on him, and perhaps others, to never have an outlet for his fetish obsessions?

I am writing this letter directly to you after watching your great talk show on television. I am with you 100% in your quest to prove your point. Good for you. I heard about you while you were still in Thornhill. I heard you are good at dealing with special needs and wants. I had intended to try to visit you before, but due to my lapses I was too late. After your show I was really pleased to realize that you were head of the Sissy Maid Academy, and I got your address out of one of the fetish magazines. I am writing to see if you would deal with a special student.

This letter is sincere, honest and comes from the real core of my heart. It's true to the word. I am fifty-two, going on twelve. I am six feet tall, 170 pounds, with brown hair, blue eyes and boyish skin. I am self employed. I spent my childhood from ages five to thirteen under the loving but very strict rule of my mother and her twin sister, Aunt Vicky. I am originally from England, but recall very little of it. We left when I was five. I recall very little of my father, who was killed in an industrial accident when I was four. Mom and Vicky and I came to Canada, where they bought a small farm outside of Guelph, Ontario. Both were avid horsewomen, and I have always had horses.

I sold the farm ten years ago after Mom died and Aunt Vicky moved to Florida. Anyway, Mom was a nurse and Aunt Vicky a teacher. She eventually would up as the principal of a Junior School near Guelph. I have always found it fascinating how one's young life moulds needs and fetishes later on in life. I was raised with lots of love and rewards, but also the kind of discipline that the world needs a lot more of today. Being British, they were true believers in "smack bum" for boys who misbehaved. Mom was six feet tall with long dark hair and Aunt Vicky was just a little shorter, with short blond hair. So what had to be done was done, and worst of all was being held and the underpants drawn down and put over the big thighs while they wore nylons, held helpless and spanked. And I mean spanked! The most embarrassing of all was being held over Mom's lap and seeing Aunt Vicky sitting on the couch, her arms folded, her big legs crossed, her high heel dangling on her toes, nodding her approval.

With Mom being a nurse and working shifts, I was often under Aunt Vicky's authority, and by my late adolescence I knew she was kinky and loved to spank. I guess my being available gave her the chance to do what she was not allowed to do at school. I got away with nothing and there were no warnings or second chances, ever. If I was naughty, she spanked my bottom, pure and simple. Up until ten years of age all I knew was the hand and the leather slipper. At ten she baptized me to the perils of the ivory hairbrush. I still have the actual brush and, if you like, you can use it on me. Never have I felt stings and bites quite like that. If I live to be one hundred, I will never forget her saying, "Young man, consider yourself lucky. If I had my way you would have got this two years ago." I tried everything to get off her lap, but she was too big and strong. When I looked in the mirror later I could see my bright red bum.

I have suffered a lot of embarrassment in my life and I may as well be honest. I am not well endowed in the male department, and am uncut. I keep it appropriately hairless. I have a real fetish for big, strong women with big legs, wearing tan stockings, especially with black seams and high heels. I wish for very severe spankings from such women. Mom wore tan stockings, but she never pulled her skirt or dress up. Both she and Aunt Vicky wore stockings, not pantyhose.

When Aunt Vicky had me alone I always tried to cover my little male parts, but my hands were always taken away and held with the humiliation of her saying something like "No young man, I have seen lots of these little things before and I have changed your diaper. Yours is not a big deal, nor will it ever be." She was right.

One time she had two of her lady friends over for dinner and she spanked me in front of them. Worst of all, after my pajama bottoms were off she held me so they could see "it". I was going on thirteen, and never had pubic hair until I was fifteen. I was never so humiliated. When Mom wasn't around she would find any excuse to spank me. She always pulled her dress right back and I could see her big thighs, brown nylon tops and always the seams at the back of her stockings. She never wore the stockings with the seams when Mom was around. She would always turn her left foot inward so I could see the seam up her leg. She always held my right hand but my left hand could touch her leg and she obviously wanted that. She would often pant as she spanked.

Since twenty-one years of age I have sought out dominant and mature females who would give me what I needed, and dress the proper way. As you see in the photos, I too like to wear tan stockings. If I am of interest I would love to hear from you and if we meet I would like a very severe spanking. I can take a really severe spanking, but I need it very childlike, always on the bare bum. I like it over a big lap, and you can have all the mistresses present you want. I would also be willing to volunteer for you to demonstrate the proper spanking that a naughty schoolboy should have to ensure modified behavior and a well adjusted attitude. I like the loud, crisp "spat, spat" that only bare wood on the bare bum can give. I love to really kick, so I may have to be restrained. I am not into sex or anything you do not agree with, but if you want to really discipline, I need it. Okay?

I do hope to hear from you, but please be discreet with the envelope. In a small town like mine everyone knows everyone.

I wrote back and said I could accommodate him, and told him what it would cost. He wrote his second letter, a long rambling letter, again in his own hand. He probably did not keep a copy of his first letter, and repeated much of what he said there, so I edited that out.

Thank you for your reply letter. Believe me, it's a real pleasure to know that there are still some real and honest people left out there. That embarrassing but honest letter I wrote to you was sincere and from my heart. I see yours that way too. There are damn few of us left. I think letters are a great way to really get to know each other, so there are no surprises in the first personal encounter.

I was really pleased to hear that "over the knee" was your specialty. As a boy it was for me the rule, not an option. I was also pleased that your favorite tool was the hairbrush as I have vivid memories of it used on me while over Aunt Vicky's lap. I'll bet you really know how to use it, like she did. I know and want to find out. I guarantee you I will not be a one time student of yours. I will call.

Right now I am doing a job in a small town in Ontario for three or four weeks. After that I will be doing one in Toronto for about six months. The coming three or four weeks will let the heat cool down for me, so to speak.

I hope you really kick the government over this. They always have their nose where it shouldn't be, and I hope they get a real lesson from you. Don't you dare give up, ever. I have enclosed a little token for you. It is not much but every little bit helps. I will send a token for every letter you write. If you want more just say so. Okay? When you did your television talk show I was hoping to see one of your crossed legs and your high heel dangling on your toe, but I'm sure I will get to see this in reality. I do not want to take up a lot of your time, but I will write a little scenario for you. It may help you better understand my feelings.

I am brought to Ms. Bedford, the Headmistress of the boys' training school by two of her female teachers, one holding each arm. I am sobbing and struggling. You are wearing a black full skirt, white blouse, tanned seamed stockings and black pumps. Your big legs are crossed. At twelve, I am totally dismayed. "Well young man, I guess being lenient with you is not the answer. Putting you over my knee and using my hand on your bare bum has obviously not gotten results, has it?" Then I say "Yes Ms. Bedford, yes it did, please." Then you say "No, it didn't. But today we will get results. Strip him ladies." Then you get up and go to your desk and take out a wooden hairbrush. You order me to be taken to the punishment room. You lead the way. I am hauled behind, getting a good look at your swaying skirt, big legs and clicking high heels. A chair is in the middle of the room and you sit on it. You order the teachers to hold me down on your lap. The teachers giggle at your mention how small my member is. You pull back your skirt and administer the brush brutally while the teachers hold me and giggle. You spank me until my bum is red and then order the teachers to restrain me on a table. When this is done you take a strap off the wall and use it mercilessly while the teachers watch and laugh.

Take care, Terri. Oh, could I please have photo of you. I swear to God no one will ever see it.

CHAPTER 4

Make Me Your Slave

I tried a number of experiments. I advertised for a live-in slave. He would clean, do laundry, shop, do errands and so forth. He would also pay rent. In return he would get a few sessions per week and of course have the pleasure of being my slave and that of the other doms. It was a great deal for a guy between jobs or recently retired. One guy was a middle age executive who got a settlement when he was let go and said for tax reasons he wanted to take a couple of years off and the arrangement suited him. We had plenty of offers and tried a few guys. Only a couple of them worked out. For the rest it was pay as you go.

* * *

Down on my knees I am submitting my slave application for your kind consideration.

I am thoroughly indoctrinated in female supremacy. Men are merely inferior species created to serve females and satisfy their needs. Men are nothing more than play toys or foot stools for females.

I do believe that men should be femininely attired to remind them of their inferior identity. I feel most comfortable wearing a bra (with breast inserts), garter belt, stockings, maxi pad and high heels. I also enjoy wearing panties or a silky slip over my face. Worshipping lingerie is becoming my daily ritual.

Dear Mistress, please help me to develop the ultra subservient nature within my inner self. I know my life will not be fulfilled without intensive slave training. I am just like a boat drifting aimlessly on water searching for the real meaning of servitude.

I am relinquishing all my rights as a creature. I am totally surrendering to you. Please subjugate me, torment me and degrade me. No service is too prurient, no punishment is too severe.

Please let me know that I am worthy of being underneath your spiked heels. I believe that I may be able to assist you in training new mistresses and slaves, or with your research projects, or in entertaining your guests.

*   *   *

Mistress, I am your most unworthy and miserable dog and undeserving of the privilege of being your property. If you will forgive my impertinence, I do most humbly beg for permission to grovel and worship at your feet and I beg to be trained as your slave.

Mistress, if you will generously grant my request, I will need to be very strictly disciplined and frequently punished. Any humiliation that you might care to impose on such a worthless slave would be more than I deserve.

You may first wish to train me to clean the floor and you will perhaps, ensure that I do this diligently by spitting on the floor and allowing me to lick it up. You may then train me as your personal slave to serve you and attend to your every whim.

You will obviously expect your slave to obey instantly when you snap your fingers and you will be completely intolerant of the slightest mistake. No doubt you will need to apply the whip regularly to such a lazy and stupid slave as I and you will expect me to lick your heels and beg forgiveness whenever I displease you.

Mistress, you will surely find that I am still too disobedient and disrespectful and will deem it necessary to impose much more strict and severe discipline on me.

You would then put a collar around my neck and lead me on a chain to the dungeon where I would be heavily bound with straps and chains, nipple clamps, a cock and ball restrainer and perhaps a colonic device. You would then proceed to instruct me very harshly in your requirements for slaves and you would make me crawl to you and cringe at your feet, begging for punishment if I wish to remain as your property.

You might then gag me, chain me to the flogging stool and give me a taste of the whip so that I may contemplate the punishment to follow. You would then put a hood on me and retire to change, at your leisure, into a fabulous black leather outfit and beautiful, thigh high, high heeled, shiny black leather boots.

When you return Mistress, you would remove the hood and then tease and torment me before thrashing me soundly on my back side. You might then move me to a suspended position and whip me with a bull whip. You would then remove the hood and then tease and torment me before thrashing me soundly on my back side. You might then move me to a suspended position and whip me with a bull whip. You would then remove the gag and permit me to beg for mercy if I promise to lick clean every inch of your boots.

After releasing me, you might humiliate me further before I am actually permitted to worship at your booted heel. You might let me lick your spittle again or perhaps I could lick your soiled underwear. When you are satisfied that I have been totally degraded, you would order me to crawl to you on the throne and allow me the ultimate privilege of licking your boots until they are perfectly spotless and gleaming.

If you are pleased with your boots, you may then strap me to the table and tease my cock and my balls until I achieve the final reward.

*   *   *

It is a privilege and honor for me to address you. I would like to apply for a position as your personal slave. At the present time I work at a bar in a small town in Alberta. I am a waiter and I clean the place. I am sending you my picture taken a few years back. I am deeply sorry, but it is the only picture I have to send you. I am good looking, as you can see on my picture and I am healthy, obedient, and loyal and a very good and hard worker. I am very trustworthy and reliable. At this time in my life I need a mistress. All my life I have missed having one. Now I am choosing to fully and meaningfully live my life as the wonderful slave I am. I hope you like my picture and the person I am, because what you read in this letter is true and very sincere. I hope to be considered for this meaningful position.

*   *   *

I propose the following science fiction or fantasy as a background scenario for our session together.

We are both powerful leaders of separate countries with wealth, power and armies to lead and slaves to command. Our countries are in natural conflict because yours is ruled by women and mine is ruled by men. Recently, I captured you, intending to make you a collared and branded slave girl as I have done to many others. However you escaped and, vowing revenge, have decided to capture me.

You have several options. For one, you could kill me. But that would be too easy. There is no fun in that. You would like to see me degraded and humiliated and experience what I have done to others. Another option is if you simply make me a slave and put me in prison I might escape, return to my country, and then have revenge on you. A third option is for you to use a device to transform me into a female slave and I lose everything. Escape to where? I would just be a collared and branded slave girl, unrecognizable as my former self to anyone. All my power is gone. If I am trained for servitude and feminized then I will owe my existence to the generosity of my new mistress. In this way you have complete victory over your enemy.

You chose the last option. I have been drugged, kidnapped and taken to your castle. I awake having been transformed into a young female. Some of my memories have been erased. I am collared and wear the clothing allowed a slave. I am heavily bound with little movement possible. I am blindfolded. I have not yet discovered my new body.

Mistress enters the room to see if her new slave has awoken. Your new slave will not accept her new role very easily. She does not know where she is or what has happened to her body. In her mind she is used to being dominant. She will struggle until she accepts this as futile.

She must be branded on the thigh with perhaps a pretty flower design so that she and all others will know she is not free and will always be a slave. Your new slave will look pretty in earrings and you should have her ears pierced. This will make her feel more feminine. She must never remove the earrings or she will be punished. She is given a feminine name to distinguish her from other slaves and which she can acknowledge as her own.

She can be hobbled if her feet become accustomed to wearing high heels. They may remain on for whatever part of the session Mistress desires. If appropriate, Mistress may wish to lock them on overnight.

She may receive dildo training. In this way she acknowledges her gender and learns her fate if she does not obey Mistress. She may also be thrown to male slaves for their use. After all, this is what she had planned in her previous life for her Mistress. This might be her ultimate fate if something should happen to Mistress.

She learns to accept that she is far happier serving Mistress than any activity she had in a past life. She might be given a chance to attend school. Although she will love the opportunity to wear a school uniform, she will probably not be a very satisfactory student and domestic training might be better. Mistress probably does not want too intelligent a slave. As a maid she will do the chores Mistress desires.

Of course she must be taught to appreciate the generosity of her new Mistress and worship her Mistress as required.

*   *   *

This client saw photos and a profile of my "glamazon" Contessa Cintra on my Web site and asked specifically for her for his session.

I am looking forward to my session with The Contessa. I would be happy to meet with her before to discuss the session if she would like. Perhaps you would share this note with her.

As to my interests and experience, as a submissive I've always been into bondage (medium to heavy), fantasy role-play, and fetish wear on both mistress and slave. I can take hoods and gags, nipple clamps (light), severe cock and ball restraint, suspension, sensory deprivation and some punishment with whip or paddle. I have a strong fetish for sheer seamed stockings on the mistress, combined with tight latex or PVC. I prefer the mistress to be heavily made up, and have a certain elegance and glamour.

As a slave I like to be dressed and restrained in latex, and to be subject to prolonged arousal training. I like being hooded, as I find the sense of being reduced to a faceless and anonymous sex-object highly erotic. I'm very visual in what I respond to, and I love the element of ritual in good bondage and discipline play. I have no interest in anal play, golden showers, smoking, marks or any unsafe practices whatsoever.

Here is a fantasy outline, picking up some of these themes, which we could use if it appeals to you.

The Contessa has bought a new slave. He kneels naked in a reception room where she inspects him, magnificent in seamed stockings, extreme high heels, long gloves and a skin tight black PVC dress. Without her permission he becomes aroused, a major act of disobedience. She determines to teach him a lesson he will not readily forget: he will be kept as her latex sex slave, in a state of helpless arousal, until he learns true obedience. He will become a faceless and anonymous sexual object, existing only to fulfill the Contessa's desires and fantasies.

First, his cock and balls are severely restrained. Then he is hooded, and dressed in latex from head to toe. Collar, cuffs and chains are added to further restrict his movement. Finally, high heeled shoes are strapped on his feet. His old identity thus removed, the slave is forced to serve the Contessa, following her commands as best he can, fetching and carrying, straightening her seams, polishing her shoes and so on. Every so often she makes sure that his cock is still rigidly erect in its restraints.

But she is still not satisfied with his performance and decides that something more severe is required. She takes the slave to a dungeon cell and prepares him for punishment. Now gagged and in severe bondage, he can only watch helplessly as she alternately whips him and caresses him into helpless arousal with a gloved hand or the touch of a nylon stocking or a glimpse of her superb breasts. Different punishments follow, each reinforcing the cycle of arousal and its painful consequences.

This, she explains, is how his life as her slave will be until he learns some self-control. Relief, if ever granted, will be strictly when and how she decides, and when not required for training he will be kept in a cage.

He did have his session with the Contessa, much like he described it. However she told him that during the session he would wear a cock ring to ensure he did not orgasm. The rules of the house, and the law as we best understood it, were that a client could only relieve themselves, by themselves, after the session. Go figure.

*   *   *

Here is a brief description of my fantasy. I am on a date at a beautiful woman's house. She proposes doing something "different". She wants to tie me to the bed and "have fun". I accept. As soon as I am firmly tied to the bed she puts a ball gag in my mouth and a hood over my head. She then puts nipple clamps on me and leaves the room without a word. She comes back soon after dressed in leather and high heels and tells me that I am now her slave toy for as long as she wants. In future, whenever I visit her, I am always kept in bondage or restraint and forced to perform foot and body worship, kept in sensory deprivation, tortured mildly by tickling, pinching or slapping or used as a model for her to show off her bondage techniques to other mistresses.

In my sessions I like heavy bondage as much as possible, and for prolonged periods. I want to be tortured (but not severely) while helpless. I also like foot and body worship. It is important that the mistress wears leather, rubber or PVC from head to toe, if possible.

I am very straight and don't want to be seen or touched by a man. Do not leave burns or scars, but you can leave welts or bruises so long as they heal within a week or so. No brown or golden showers.

*   *   *

This client's letter had to be heavily edited and rewritten. He also had great difficulty communicating in person, meaning that to get his true feelings and desires out in the open, very difficult for most men at the best of times, was exceptionally awkward.

I am e-mailing you to explain my feelings and desires. If it is possible and you agree I would like my next several visits to be test visits where I have the opportunity to explore and expand my limits to new heights. To really live life and feel alive one must visit the edge of their endurance and fears and have the tremendous feeling of and satisfaction of doing something that was a real thrill and being able to say they did it. The satisfaction and excitement I get from doing something I would be embarrassed to do or afraid to do is so immense that I live with a rush for several days. I ask you again that for the next several visits you challenge and test my endurance, fears and embarrassment. Some ideas for my test: (1) forty-five minutes in a straitjacket with arms behind my back and standing in high heels, (2) two hours in a coffin in tight bondage, (3) to be locked out of your house for many hours and must find places to go and get business cards [*he mentioned several local fetish clothing and equipment merchants*], (4) to be made to wear laced up boots for an entire visit (5) to be made to stand in heels for an entire visit (6) one hundred strokes with three or four different instruments.

*   *   *

I arrive in just a few days. Both my excitement and dread are growing. Speaking with you was a pleasure. You have quite a pleasant voice, almost soothing. I imagine however this can be in some contrast to the aura you are capable of in appropriate circumstances. Handing one over to someone new and unknown offers its own addition to the adventure, but it also introduces some real anxiety. There is a lot of trust involved. Speaking with you seemed to give me much greater confidence and allowed me to savor the "fun" anxiety.

You mentioned several accommodation options. Unfamiliar with any, I would like to get a taste of each, perhaps. I think I would desire to sleep and spend most time, in normal or feminine environments, but with frequent visits to the dungeon or punishment rooms. Your choice and my surprise!

This letter is intended as an introduction, to give you some advance knowledge of me, my limits and desires. I hope that it will help you, offering a starting point for an arrival interview and triggering your imagination as you contemplate my fate.

I am fifty-six years old, six feet tall with a moderate belly in need of a corset. I have been actively playing for a couple of years, having sessions with three individual doms and three dungeons with multiple doms. Most experience has been with a Los Angeles mistress/dungeon where I have stayed for a five day span as well as several extended six to eight hour sessions. Almost all my sessions are three or more hours. I have tolerated several "moderate" beatings, as described, by doms who give very severe ones as well. I'm not at the extremes, but fairly tolerant and adventurous.

[*Here he offered a reference adding*] I hesitate to offer this contact as she might well offer suggestions or requests I'd regret, but she knows me quite well.

My health is good but I have a disk and nerve issue in the neck and right shoulder. Please don't suspend me by the arms or keep my arms overhead. I have had a small heart attack and am on some medication for it. There is no risk or limit from this though. I had a physical last week complete with blood tests, and all was good.

My limits are basically safe and sane, meaning no permanent harm, marks or noticeable changes (such as shaving). My ass can be lightly marked and you can leave bruises that will clear in a few days and until then can be covered by underwear.

In my sessions you should emphasize vulnerability, discipline, humiliation, restraints, sissy slave and cross-dressing as humiliation. Within that I ask that my genitals be unprotected, with weights on my balls and perhaps a leash. Every moment with my hands shackled behind me is a treasure, but because of my shoulder it is best this be done with leather cuffs connected a few inches apart.

*   *   *

Things to do to your slave: hard trampling, jump as hard as you can on me (mostly two at a time), jump off things on to me, trample my head, step on and off my neck, have one mistress smother me while another jumps me, and do all the above in a competition among the mistresses to see who can make me submit. Please do not wear shoes, as they leave marks. I will tap the floor if I need you to stop. Thank you. Your carpet, Stomp.

CHAPTER 5

Make Me a Sissy Maid

Sissy Maid is the term used for a slave who is feminized and compelled to do domestic chores. The man becomes a subservient woman. It is a complete gender switch (in terms of traditional gender roles) for a man who is almost always not gay. The fantasy was basically to be a maid slave to a powerful woman or group of powerful women. It was an excuse to cross-dress and look at the adored dominant woman. It was a basis for punishment and humiliation. Thus the sissy maid scenarios simultaneously combined fetishism, cross-dressing, masochism and voyeurism, among other things.

* * *

Thank you for your quick reply. You definitely sound like it's worth a visit. But it would be a long journey so I would like a longer stay. It would also better enable me to "get into character". I was thinking of a one week stay. Is there a possibility of that? What would the cost be?

You state I will receive a proper Victorian education. I am not sure of the meaning of this but take it to mean being a Victorian maid. Actually as a transvestite I don't seek so much of a natural look, but rather the very feminine look of the nineteen fifties, meaning either very tight or very billowing skirts, high heels, bouffant hairdos (I have long hair) and so forth. I see you offer classes in manicures and hair care. My role model is the American housewife of the nineteen fifties with apron, petticoats, scarves and so forth.

But the most important thing for me is the experience of feeling under control and being pressured and forced to make that extra effort and take that extra step toward my feminization that I don't dare take myself. I feel confident you will be the woman for this.

As much as I would love to acquire maid skills, I would also love to experience being an elegant lady, perhaps even experience another of my dreams which is being the bride in full attire and fully made up with long finger nails, hair done up, false eyelashes and so forth. Perhaps you can even cooperate with a beauty salon so I could experience the "full treatment".

*   *   *

Thank you for your reply Headmistress. It is good to know that your school remains to train boys to be useful. Your Web site mentions flexibility in your training programs. I would like to discuss the possibility of a somewhat specialized regimen within your program. I believe it is best for me to receive petticoat discipline, punishment and sissy maid training. That is, I should present myself for discipline, punishment and training, not for my "pleasure". The regimen should be strict and include corporal punishment of a strict nature. Please let me know if such a regimen is possible. Thank you.

*   *   *

I am seriously interested in attending your Academy. Specifically I am seeking serious, professional maid training, combined with corporal punishment (especially caning). I have a little maid training and plenty of punishment training, and need to sincerely and genuinely become a competent, well trained, truly feminine and disciplined maid. I have found that the combination of rigorous training, extensive housework, punitive chores, punishments, caning, detention, large quantities of lines [*writing out lines as punishment*], extended corner standing, mouth soaping and the like work wonders. I would like to enquire about the possibility of this under your gracious, serious and strict supervision for a period of some consecutive days if this is to your liking. Please let me know if this is suitable and appropriate.

*   *   *

I would like to spend my life as a slave and surrender my will, heart and soul to you for life. You can have complete ownership of me. You can run the ass off me and be as aggressive, rough and demanding as you wish. You will be in command of me twenty-four seven and I will be your sissy slave.

I will obey you on my knees at all times. I will be your own sissy slave for life. I will live in a sissy maid's room under lock and key, sleeping on rubber sheets with my non-removable collar on, all alone and helpless. You can keep me in chains or handcuffs at night or during the day too. You can use belts and straps on me. I trust you with all my heart. You can use me to make money.

I will be perfectly obedient and no matter how hard you are on me I will know it is love for your sissy maid.

*   *   *

Thank you so much for that nice letter. I am now not only impressed with your Web site, I am impressed that you took the time to write me such a thoughtful letter.

I can no longer control my girl urges, which have been life-long. Your letter let me know you understand people like me. Whether or not you respond to this letter I just feel the need to talk to someone who really understands, and I won't keep writing you. I promise. I just need to get some feelings out in a forum that is not primarily dominated by sex. I think you probably know where I am coming from. I guess I am writing you because there might be some wisdom that you could pass on to me, maybe not, and so maybe this is a shot in the dark. I'll do my best to make it concise and tell it like it is. Here we go.

I have been married for seven years. I am a young looking forty and it is the first marriage for both of us. My wife and I don't have intercourse. The last time was over three years ago. Neither of us feels the need any more. In her case she has a medical condition that renders her pretty asexual. I dated girls prior to marriage, and had two broken engagements because I was not passionate enough. When one of those girls would get a new boyfriend I would masturbate thinking about what he was going to do to her. I do masturbate three times a week with my large dildo, and my wife is just fine with that, but at the same time admits that it doesn't do much for her. Yet she still wants me to do it and gets kind of mad if I don't because she says I get "out of balance if I don't masturbate as a sissy".

My wife is really a soul mate for me, and we are great friends, a real support system in life. My wife works outside the home and I help her with that, even though I am also employed. I do most of the 'maid services" for her in our very nice home and love that role.

I dress as my sissy self every evening, and wear work clothes during the day that either a man or woman could wear. My wife is genuinely very comfortable with my female side and even says to me that she married me for this. She even buys me special clothes from time to time, and recently made me a cute black skirt. I will never leave this woman. We are partners in life and have a deep spiritual bond. Yet, I am at a point in life where I know I can't stop my need to be feminized a little more. I feel so much like a girl that I don't even feel I need hormones, but would love to take them. Yet, at the same time, I am willing to keep a little masculinity to please my wife from time to time, although she really is comfortable with me en femme all of the time.

I guess I am wondering several things. First of all, do you think most sissy maids would masturbate? Or, have they had enough hormones to eliminate that urge? I do feel the need to purge the male hormones in me, and that release is always the reward for letting my female sexuality have its way. I know I can be content for life being a masturbator, so long as those close to me know that and kind of bless it. Am I strange? Secondly, how might the Millicent Farnsworth Sissy Maid Academy help me? Does my story kind of eliminate me as a candidate? I know my "Mistress", my wife, is never bothered by me being more of a sissy, because it always makes me a better servant, and she just loves that. She has helped me with makeup and bought me lots of it.

When I wrote to you the first time everything I said was true, but I was kind of allowing myself to live the fantasy of being a full time sissy maid in some manner. That would be very nice and, had I not married, who knows? But I do genuinely love my soul mate, my Mistress who knows me, and just brings out the girl in me. I want to be the best girl for her in the world.

*   *   *

As per your instructions, I humbly submit this formal letter of introduction. As we have already had discussions concerning various topics, I will proceed to verbalize my thoughts, hopes and fears, while also detailing some historical background. I was born on June 5, 1960, the fourth child of five, two boys, three girls. Do I wish I were the fourth girl? Sometimes I wonder. I had a fairly normal upbringing in a secure suburban environment, until my parents divorced when I was a lad of ten. Within a few years, with little or no male guidance, I found myself discovering sexuality by searching my oldest sister's lingerie drawer, borrowing panties and pantyhose to enhance my juvenile masturbatory habits.

This fascination of feminine things so smooth, sensual and silky has stayed with me for life. By the time I was in the eighth grade, I knew I was growing, or not growing, in the manner of the other boys, both in tastes, preferences and physical body maturity. While my peers were discovering the joys of sprouting breasts on our female classmates, I began to fixate on the beauty of their feet. A girl named Jane Doe used to sit right in front of me and often wore yellow socks with brown clogs (very popular in the early to mid seventies). To this day I always get excited when observing superior females wearing clogs. I also instantly glance down whenever I see females to observe what type of footwear they have chosen to grace their lovely feet with.

Upon entering high school, other boys were passing me by in the maturation process. I was fourteen, then fifteen, skinny and underdeveloped, especially in the genital department. This caused me great embarrassment, which I would ironically turn later in my adult life to a main driver of arousal and humiliation. I made it out of high school with a miserable dating record, due in part to my lack of confidence regarding my smallish body and also a growing submissive attitude towards all women. I went into the workforce in the late nineteen seventies and had my first session with a pro dom a year later. I was completely transformed: stockings, panties, full slip, bra, wig, dress, shoes and some makeup. There would be no turning back.

I basically bounced around in different jobs in the early nineteen eighties, never quite finding my niche in life, except for one semi-enjoyable job. In the middle nineteen eighties I was hired as an assistant manager of a women's shoe store. Yummy! I loved that job in many respects, especially when the customers were powerful and bossy. I left, however, after two years or so and still miss the subservient nature of that particular period.

Shortly before the decade ended I was about to embark on a major rebuilding program in my life, a reclamation project that has now been going on for the last decade or so. At that point I was a nobody with not much to offer anyone. I was about to finally mature and set goals for my life, and begin to truly grow.

Ten years ago I was hired by the company I now work for, a major corporation. Ten years of stability, good earnings and the opportunity to get my college education have enabled me to be in the position I now find myself in. I feel I have much to offer a young lady with respect to suitability of a mate, but for the fact I am completely unsuited to provide for her adult, female sexual needs. My complete lack of experience in the normal sexual arena with females has made me now realize that this facet of life experience is never going to avail itself to me. I therefore have concluded that being a chastised, feminized maid to a powerful woman is preferable to spending the rest of my life alone. Serving a woman who I would love to date but realistically have zero chance to do so would be the most fulfilling assignment imaginable to this lifelong sissy wimp.

Over the last two decades I have accumulated outfits and uniforms (cheerleader, maid, ballerina, etc.), oodles of feminine under things, and saw many a dominatrix. I have been photographed and published in S&M magazines, been publicly dominated and humiliated at parties, and would consider myself very experienced in the realm of the submissive male. The question before me now arises, am I ready to take my sissy sexuality to a higher level, one of thinking, acting and behaving as a submissive female? That answer is obviously yes!

I realize that due to my thoroughly submissive nature (which manifests itself in everyday interactions with women I meet, and immediately turns them off to me as a prospective mate), along with my lack of any sexual confidence whatsoever resulting from my boyish genitalia, has made me a perfect candidate for perfect emasculation, feminization and perfect slavery. I therefore humbly submit this application to Headmistress for proper training at her Academy. Perhaps I can learn enough and progress to the point of being worthy of Your Highness recommending me to a beautiful, powerful woman to serve in such a capacity for the remainder of my life.

He concluded his letter with a physical description of himself and payment and travel details.

*   *   *

Here is the story of a man who most would call normal and successful. He was a very impressive looking man, well dressed and with a good job. As he says, and as he later told me, he was father to three children who lived with his divorced wife. In that role he paid his alimony and participated in raising the kids. It was only after his marriage ended that he discovered a self he never knew. Note the lapses of time. I'll have another word or two to say when he is finished.

It was with a great sense of emotion and relief that I read of your academy in June 1999. Let me try to explain why I was so overwhelmed and amazed when I saw your article. I'll start out by saying I have had some training by a dom, and just remembering how it made me feel to serve and worship and, yes, even be corrected for disobedience, brought tears to my eyes. You see, this dom/sub relationship occurred from 1982 to 1985, when my mistress moved to Alberta. We kept up communication for a while, but over time it became less and less and gradually we lost contact. The reason I never followed her was that I have three children from an earlier marriage, that I felt I must be around for. I don't regret that decision.

Until recently I suppressed all of these feelings, but over the last year I have started to attend some fetish nights here in Toronto. As well I am seeing pro doms from time to time. While I found these avenues to be very satisfying, there was still a void. The reason is that I was trained mostly in domestic service, as well as personal duties. I have found it difficult to find anyone who specializes in this field. As a result, when I read about your academy and sent for and got the information package, the emotions just overwhelmed me and I just had to meet you.

Please understand, I'm not trying to relive an old fantasy, but look forward to further training and education. To better understand me, I'll give you a brief resume. I first met what was to become my mistress, back in 1982, in a small town near Toronto when I moved to the same apartment building. She lived across the hall. After knowing her some months I finally worked up the nerve to ask her out. I didn't think of it becoming a dom/sub relationship, but I found on our dates that she was very bossy, and I found that a turn on.

She eventually told me she attended fetish parties at a well known venue in Toronto. She filled me in on the scene and asked me if I would attend as her sub. I agreed, and the more she told me the more curious I became. It was agreed that because she "wore the pants", I must wear the panties, so I attended fetish night dressed in baby clothes and frilly panties.

To make a very long story short, after the first fetish night I agreed to become her domestic slave. She had me agree to certain rules. I was always to wear what was asked of me. My limits would be respected, but they would be expanded. When in training I would always address her as Mistress (*he gave her real name*). I would be punished for jobs not well done, and rewarded as my mistress saw fit.

Over time I was trained in cleaning, doing laundry, drawing baths, other domestic chores and being the maid at parties my mistress hosted. At these parties I would be expected to serve drinks, tidy up, keep ash trays clean and even provide foot massages and polish the boots of guests—sometimes when the women wore them.

The following is a typical party at which I was a maid. I would of course be dressed in a maid's outfit as I greeted guests, hung up their coats and so forth. I would show them to their seats and make sure they had drinks, snacks or cigarettes. If something was amiss I would be punished in front of the guests. This would include such things as being made to stand in the corner or to bend over a coffee table and be spanked. If a guest did not have a drink in front of them or some other comfort did not meet their expectation, the mistress would even ask them to suggest a punishment. As you can imagine, over the number of parties there were several unusual ones.

As time went on I was quite well trained in the following areas: hostess, laundress, cleaner, masseuse, bathing assistance and dresser. As I mentioned earlier, there is a deep seeded need in me to serve, to obey and try my best to please my mistress and those around her.

I hope you will agree to see me.

He married early and after he divorced and got his own place he met the lady across the hall. Although he went to doms and eventually to me, it appeared that those few years in the 1980's were the highlight of his life, and nothing since has come close. That's probably because he had his outlet on a regular basis, probably after suppressing his feelings while married and prior. With the lady across the hall he did not have to pay. It would be prohibitively expensive to do so, with all the details in place. It is interesting to see, when they look back many years, which relationships men remember most fondly. He told me he knew many women since then, but he said the lady across the hall spoiled him for any other woman.

* * *

I will go by whatever name you choose. Public outings are a lot of fun. I've gone out in a couple of different ways: one as a cross-dressed woman going to various places, the other dressed in a sissy type outfit or a couple of articles of sissy clothing mixed with my male attire as forced humiliation or punishment. In this scenario the headmistress or whoever is supervising me doesn't accompany me directly, but observes from a distance that I do as I was instructed to (no need to embarrass anyone but me).

My female persona is a very submissive sissy maid, although I like to reach this point by being dominated and disciplined by my superior(s), being told what I will wear, how I will behave, how to serve and being brought down from my normal male persona to the lowest submissive of female roles—the sissy maid.

I have been involved for twenty years in this role and have become very, very submissive when "forced" into it (although of course I love it). Your school is the best outlet that I have found that suits my needs so totally. I can't help but wonder how you can understand my deepest needs so well. Everything on your Web site looks great to me. Although in my everyday life I am always submissive to women, when I'm put into my sissified state my submission deepens tremendously and the more direction and discipline I get the more submissive I become. I crave being completely controlled by the Headmistress and anyone she delegates, for my entire stay.

Things that could be of benefit to me with your sissy maid course include: immersion in my sissy persona, complete submission, a chance to serve women (and men, if instructed to do so by the Headmistress), being chained and punished (sounds silly, but I crave corporal punishment), being given repetitive tasks and so forth. I would also like to be made to wear diapers and pretty girl clothes.

* * *

This is "Rachel" writing to make a confession. After visiting your Academy in May I thought I was an experienced sissy maid and some sort of a big deal. I went to visit a dom who advertised, thinking I was quite a girl about town. Then in October I went to see another advertiser still thinking I am an experienced fetish person.

I must tell you Headmistress, I was entirely wrong. These sessions were, without a doubt, extremely enjoyable, but they did not offer me the long term guidance and instruction that I obviously need. Headmistress, I strongly and sincerely apologize. I was a fool! I thought I could move on and try other things.

Headmistress Millicent, I must now get on my knees and beg you to accept me back. I would only hope that you would grant me the concession of having me back to the Academy again so I can show you my gratitude and dedication to the sissy maid lifestyle. It is not your approval I need Headmistress, but your forgiveness for straying from what I know I was born for. That is to serve you, your clients or your guests, as they were meant to be served. I sincerely apologize for my indiscretions, and truly hope that I may be offered a second chance.

Headmistress, I have so much to learn that I pray I am allowed to visit you again. I will allow you a sacrifice of whatever you deem fit, if you allow me this privilege. Thank you so much Headmistress.

*   *   *

I am not sure your school could help me but I live in hope. I have read all of the material on your site and find it very exciting but I am also a bit shy. My desire is to be a complete sissy maid or panty maid to a mistress and/or master. I wish to serve them totally with erotic full body massages, baths, dressing, everything. I wish to look after their private desires totally and to be subject to their total inspection at all times, no matter where I am, by them and their friends. I am very submissive and this is a very lustful sexual thing for me.

Would your classes help me to master the art of total body servitude, including oral techniques to the sexual fulfillment of my mistress and/or master? What exercises or classes would I be able to take to this end and how long would it take me to complete the course? Do you have a placement service? Thank you for your time. I look forward in hope of hearing from you.

*   *   *

I do hope this finds Headmistress in good spirits. I must confess that I am totally amazed by your wonderful and classy Web site. I can't stop looking at the wonderful range of different images of Headmistress. The same goes for the intelligent writing and descriptions of the Academy and possible experiences there.

After looking at all the lovely pages one thought covers all the others. It would be amazing to live this dream that Headmistress is offering. I am actually going to Toronto next week, and I would very much like to know the availability of Headmistress for a private class of up to a half day. I do hope it's not too blunt to ask about such an experience on [*he mentioned possible dates*]. I really like the idea of putting much energy into planning a visit to the Academy, to make the best of it. I'd naturally be glad to supply a longer letter of introduction and answer any questions Headmistress might have after reading these initial lines.

I picture many possible scenarios based on the wonderful Web page that Headmistress has created. If I would single out some particular requests those would be in the area of forced feminization by a stern Headmistress. I would like Headmistress (naturally depending on whether that would please her) to carefully transform me into a glamorous woman. I would appreciate all the details of an ultra-feminine woman, then in different ways being disciplined by Headmistress, as she desires.

If I can humbly state some wishes, they would include makeup, an area that interests me especially. It would include features like full glossy lips, long fake eyelashes and lots of tasty eye shadow, maybe the Las Vegas showgirl look, a rich bitch, like a classy Joan Collins from "Dallas or similar". The image should be glamorous, but also include some clear hints in makeup and clothing of simply being a really willing little slut there to please. Long nails with shiny nail polish are another fetish I would love to experience if Headmistress wishes me to.

When it comes to clothing, classic items like a tight lace corset and stiletto heels would be wonderful. The rest of the clothing could be chosen depending on the scenario being followed, and naturally according to the wishes of Headmistress. Large rhinestone jewellery or other similar classy female accessories could also be added according to the image Headmistress is creating for the day.

I do like the idea of a customized workshop after further discussions with Headmistress. I would for example very much like the fantasy of being transformed as above by a stern headmistress, turned into a "high class secretary", and then trained and have to perform a range of duties that might occur behind closed office doors.

There would be duties that some male egos think secretaries might just have to do because their stern female boss tells them to. Naturally they will be obedient and a quick learner, to keep their job and please the boss. The boss had long suspected that beneath the proper mincing and polite secretary image there was something much more sleazy hidden, just waiting to come out with the guidance of the stern female boss. One would naturally suspect his hidden personality based on her makeup and appearance at the office.

Another part of my fantasy would be to be carefully feminized and pampered, as Headmistress gives me the benefit of her attention for the full transformation into her own little woman doll creation.

I hope Headmistress doesn't mind me sharing the above in such a straightforward way. If Headmistress finds it necessary I will naturally change any of my ways as an obedient student applying to enter the Academy. That naturally also includes writing about fantasies exactly in the way that is most appreciated by Headmistress.

So, not to bore Headmistress, I would like to finish this e-mail for now. I have just looked at the picture of Headmistress again. I must confess that you fully encompass the image of beauty, class and femininity.

* * *

I am very interested in applying to your Academy for education so that I may become a full time live-in sissy maid for a dominant mistress. I believe completely in female supremacy and I have reviewed your Web site (many times) and I am fascinated by what you offer. I would also like to be able to provide financial assistance to my mistress's household by providing support to her business, working as a model or female impersonator, or some other activity that would require my living, as much as possible, if not full time, as a woman.

I have no limitations on my feminization and honestly believe that with the right discipline and training I could become passable. I am also 100% submissive.

I am a professional in my mid forties [*He then gave me details of his profession and education, which were quite impressive*]. I feel that I possess skills and experiences, in addition to those I might acquire at the Academy that will be beneficial to both the Mistress and the Academy. Relocation is not a problem. I can assure you that I am sincere in my desire to change my lifestyle and fully embrace both my "new" gender and role in life as a sissy maid.

*   *   *

This client visited from Scandinavia and I had to rewrite his letter almost word by word.

I have booked my flight to Toronto. It will be my first visit to your country. I will arrive in Toronto [*he gives details of his arrival*] and I ask if I can be picked up at the airport. I also wonder if you accept AMEX [*which of course we did*].

Here is a little about my wishes for my visit to your Academy. I do like to dress up. But it is also hard for me to adapt into a female role, so forced feminization is a must. I think the Charm School for Cross-Dressers is best. Things I would like to learn include: corset training, walking in high heels, makeup, sissy manners, nails, wig care, a wedding day fantasy and how to wear a ballroom dress. I also love conservative female office attire. In short, anything that would make me a perfect lady.

For punishment I want spanking, severe bondage, gags, masks, collars and general restraints. I might also want to explore giving oral servitude to another sissy. I have never done this, but I think this will improve my sissy attitude. I would love to please [*he mentioned a sissy shown on the site*], but this is for the Headmistress to decide. Can you please explain what a field trip is?

I would like to tell you a little about myself. I am a non-smoker, social drinker, go to church once a week, like to meet new friends and am involved in several outdoor activities. Feel free to ask me anything.

*   *   *

This client may have been bordering on considering a sex change. I am not sure if that is what he means here by "gender reassignment". He only visited my house once, in 1994. It was closed down soon after his visit and I did not hear from him when I reopened four years later. I got this letter a couple of weeks after he visited, which was only for one day. He did not put a return address or phone number, and this was before the Internet. He may have been from out of town and seen my ad in the trade papers. His letter is hand written. I had almost no editing to do. He mentions one of the towns a few hours from Toronto (which I have changed) that is famous for its university, so it appears he is not an unsuccessful person occupationally. However, it appears he lived in a very small town or in the countryside before that. If he lived in a big city he might have realized that his predilections were not uncommon or indicative of disorder. He was well spoken and very presentable. He is exclusively concerned with cross-dressing pure and simple, but including his letter in this chapter is more appropriate than any other.

I've been pondering over this letter now for several days. I'm not sure where to begin or how to say what I have to. I'll start at the beginning and hope that what I write here can make some sense to you and that perhaps you can help me understand. This is also why I want to see the doctor, so that I can understand what is and has been happening to me. I know you are not a therapist, but my thinking is that you have been involved with this for some time and have come across all types of people.

I have wanted to open up to someone for a very long time but have been unable to find anybody that would understand or that I could trust. Even my closest friends would never be able to understand what I feel. Things have happened to me in the past that I have told nobody about. I didn't know how to tell them and what they would think of me if I did tell.

I have a lot of secrets that have been pent up for years and you are going to be the first one to know all of them. No one knows, because I have been afraid, ashamed and embarrassed to reveal my secrets.

First, I was sexually abused as a child. There was a sitter who made me masturbate him so that he would not tell my parents I had misbehaved. I have told only one other person of this, a counselor in my home town. If I remember correctly, he was suggestive of the Clark Institute [*a major psychiatric care institution in Toronto*]. I never followed through with it.

Second, I have been cross-dressing longer than I claimed. My first recollection was when I was around thirteen or fourteen. I borrowed one of my mother's nightgowns. I don't know why I did it. I don't remember.

If I had to guess I would say it was sexually motivated. I cross-dressed through my teenage years on and off. I told no one. It was always "in the closet". I stopped for a while when I moved to Guelph [*possibly here he went to college, and had a roommate*]. I don't know why but I started again. I would wear panties and pantyhose, skirts or dresses: whatever I could find and always in private. Then I progressed into nightgowns.

I got caught once wearing a nightie. I was in bed one morning when a roommate opened my door to tell me of a phone call. He saw me in a pink nightie and broadcast to everyone what he had seen. I managed to deny it and convince everyone that he was seeing things.

I cross-dressed a couple of times in front of my now ex-wife. She didn't understand so I took it back into the closet. I did stop again for a while. After my divorce I started again, in the closet of course. Somewhere down the line it stopped being sexual. I no longer got aroused by it. I just felt more comfortable dressed as a woman than a man.

Somehow when I was with my wife I had made a remark or a dare to her and she pulled out an outfit for me to wear. She knew nothing about my cross-dressing. I wore her clothes that day, all in fun she thought. It slowly became more serious and was happening more and more. When my wife left me I cleaned out my closets thinking that was the reason she left me. I kept a few things but I'm betting that I disposed of several hundred dollars worth of clothes. I thought I might be able to stop again. As you can tell I didn't.

You asked me why I'm doing this. I believe that my honest answer would have to be that I want to become Judith. Judith is not just an escape. I think it's who I want to be. That is why your lessons are so important to me. I want to be able to look and act female. I want to see if I can pass. Would I consider the gender reassignment? I honestly don't know. If I did go through with it, my male side would disappear. I would be starting life over. Nothing would be able to remain of the old. I would have to give up my family and my friends.

I hope you understand why I tried to deceive you and please let me know that I can and will be honest from now on no matter how embarrassed I might get. At our meeting you made me feel very relaxed and comfortable. I can't explain it, but I feel that I can trust you.

* * *

This client gave very detailed responses on his questionnaire. He wrote very well. I have consolidated and adapted his comments into letter form.

I started cross-dressing like many others. My first experience came when I was about six or seven years old. Sometime while in high school I realized my fetish for stockings. I would try on my mother's lingerie whenever I got the chance. Again, I suppressed the feelings until I reached my late thirties, when I also discovered my interest in bondage and discipline and so forth. It was at that time that I also realized how significant cross-dressing fantasies were in the minds of many other submissive men. Thanks to a lot of reading I found on the Internet, I discovered two important things: I wasn't alone and there probably wasn't much I could do to suppress my feelings. So I decided to ride with it and to buy a few things in order to have some fun. Since I love the idea of forced fem, I started seeing professional mistresses on occasion in order to make fantasy a reality and to mix cross-dressing with my newfound interest in other masochistic activities. Although I will occasionally dress by myself, I usually do it in the presence of a mistress. That is where I am today! I have a few items of clothing but I really want to experience what it is like to go the whole way and to be trained in the finer points of being a sissy maid. I would also like to acquire more of a wardrobe. Now I fantasize about being the sissy maid of very dominant women, perhaps even to the point of serving them at a fetish event.

I absolutely do not go out in public cross-dressed. I have no experience at public outings and can't, at this time, imagine it being pleasurable. I am not even close to being there and I am not sure I ever will be. I would have to feel very comfortable that I am passable. This will be the first time that I will be in the presence of others (even if they are like-minded) other than with a mistress. The academy idea excites me, but I can't at this time describe a female persona for myself. However, my favorite female look is the French maid, but I would have to be led through the entire process. I can however say that rather than poise and manners training, I would prefer just to be a submissive sissy maid.

Your Academy looks like the perfect opportunity to turn fantasy into reality. From the description of your Web site it seems like you have assembled all the right tools to make this a truly memorable experience. Borrowing from the course descriptions on your site, you can help me by guiding me through the whole process starting with "Personal

Preparations" including the transformation, forced fem, chastity, uniforms and accepting punishment and discipline. Then we could focus on skills developed in the "Dressing Preparations" state like petticoat training and discipline, corset training, dressing for service, Victorian Ball Gowns and leather and lace. Throughout this period, you should administer appropriate levels of discipline to keep me focused.

Once I have attained the proper mental focus and personal skills, I would envision using future sessions to acquire those skills necessary to be a proper lady's sissy maid.

*   *   *

Thank you so much for talking with me on the phone this past Monday. It was a great feeling being able to talk with someone about a difficult subject. It proved to be one of the high points of the day. The discussion certainly posed many ideas, several of which appear below. Lack of memory on my part failed to include additional ones.

Here he went into options on pricing, citing a limited budget, and then travel arrangements and so forth.

It would be great if the day unfolded somewhat as follows. Any suggestions from you would be greatly appreciated. Perhaps a surprise or two would also be welcome.

First, enforced feminization in bra, panties, corset, stockings, chastity belt, petticoat, maid's uniform, wig, high heels and transformation (did I forget anything?)

Second, instruction is given on walking, sitting, talking, curtsying, kneeling and so forth. Modes of address, sissy attitude and rules by which sissy maids are to respect their superiors should be reviewed. Discipline and punishment for errant sissy maids is to be reviewed and demonstrated (particularly to include a spanking).

Third, role playing and private theater are listed as a lesson or option. I always wondered what it might be like to "appear" in a "play" or scene as a sissy maid with lines to deliver in front of an audience (probably a very small one which wouldn't mind laughing at or heckling a sissy maid). Have I perhaps overstated the intent or scope of this lesson?

Fourth, I should be given chores to do such as in the kitchen, possibly baking some chocolate chip brownies (if you like this possibility let me know so that the proper ingredients may be brought along) and cleaning. Perhaps teaching the sissy maid proper songs to sing may be included.

Fifth, an infraction of sissy maid etiquette is found in the performance of my duties from above. Punishment is required such as a spanking. Additionally, restraints such as handcuffs connected to leg cuffs by a chain along with a ball gag or similar gag should be worn by the sissy maid. The sissy maid is then returned to her duties. Other personnel who may see or walk by the sissy maid snicker or ask embarrassing questions. The questions are difficult for the sissy maid to answer because of her gag. In addition the sissy maid may find it difficult to satisfy certain requirements such as curtsying to others due to her restraints. Infractions are duly noted.

And sixth, noted infractions are brought to the attention of the sissy maid's mistress. The sissy maid is called to account for her infractions. A spanking may be required while the sissy maid is restrained in her handcuffs or perhaps a pillory or other such device. It may be necessary to leave the sissy maid pinioned in the pillory while other personnel at the Sissy Maid Academy are invited and encouraged to witness punishment.

It should be pointed out that I have no acting experience since third grade. Several times I have had dreams where I was supposed to act in a play and didn't have a clue what my lines were. It would be interesting to try a sketch of this sort. Despite or in spite of the above, I am not (at least not yet) involved in S&M. However the spanking and restraints have been tried and found most intriguing. [*He then gives his height, weight and measurements*].

I believe you also mentioned a snack and possibly rest period were included in the session. Again, please feel free to add suggestions. Is this too little? Is it too much? Let me know what the next step in the process is. See you on the eighth.

*   *   *

As you can imagine, if I was to stage these elaborate fantasies as written it would require a lot of time, not to mention clothes and so forth. When arranging sessions I mentioned hourly rates and other administrative things and usually suggested a pared-down version of what they were requesting. I would explain that simply dressing them and acting out a basic scenario would take half a day of a mistress's time, and that there was overhead to consider. I could always mention briefly what it would cost them to spend half a day in a lawyer's office. So when they attended they were appreciative of the time and cost elements. Most were pleased with what they experienced given what they paid. Few had enough money to fully realize their fantasies, but then, who does?

CHAPTER 6

Make Me a Baby

In my first house I did not have a "nursery", but I did in my second house. Infantilism is more popular than most people think. These men were interested in being little children. They had no sexual interest in actual children.

* * *

An adult male is turned into a very submissive baby girl. After all the adult clothes have been taken off Mistress/Mommy is in charge. Sissy Baby does not resist because he/she really enjoys being Mommy's precious little sissy baby girl. Mommy treats her little sissy and expects her sissy to act like an eight month old baby girl.

Mommy knows what sissy needs before any of sissy's diapers are pinned on. Mommy may decide that her precious sissy's little wee-wee needs to be "dressed up". Mommy may tie a ribbon snugly around the wee-wee and bag as well as cover the wee-wee with a baby bootie. Mommy knows her little sissy baby will feel some pressure against her diapers.

Mommy may decide her sissy needs an enema because sissy's bowels need to be purged quickly. Sissy baby submits to Mommy's decision by spreading her legs and raising them high in the air. Sometimes Mommy decides that one or two suppositories need to be inserted into her precious sissy's little baby bum-bum because of constipation. Mommy knows that suppositories take a little longer to work but her little sissy will have that full and need to go feeling soon enough.

Mommy may decide that her little sissy baby's bum-bum needs a dildo inserted for retention. Mommy knows her sissy will feel the dildo slide in and out as baby crawls and plunge deep inside when sissy sits down. Mommy knows her precious little baby sissy needs several very thick diapers between her legs. Mommy knows the diapers have to be pinned snugly on her sissy. The precious sissy wouldn't be able to close her legs after her diapers are pinned on. Mommy makes sure her sissy baby spreads her legs wide as the diapers are being put on. Mommy always remembers that the plastic panties are put on over the diapers. If her baby girl is lucky, Mommy will let her wear sissy pants.

Mommy decides which clothes her baby girl will wear. Sometimes, Mommy decides to put a baby dress on the sissy. Mommy knows these dresses do nothing to hide her sissy baby's diapered bottom. Sometimes sissy will wear a romper suit or sun suit. Mommy knows her precious sissy needs to wear a bonnet and booties.

Mommy knows when to give her sissy baby the bottle and when to feed her. Mommy makes sure her baby girl gets lots of fluid by feeding her several bottles. Mommy also makes sure her sissy gets enough to eat by feeding her two or more big bowls of Pabulum. The sissy baby always needs a bib when being fed because she doesn't always get all the Pabulum in her mouth.

Mommy knows her precious baby enjoys being constantly told how sissy-like and baby-like she really is. Mommy also knows her baby girl needs to have her diapers checked often for wetties. Mommy knows that sissy baby's diapers can be wet several times before changing. If sissy baby is really good, Mommy may feel baby's bottom while sissy is sitting on her lap messing her pants. If sissy has loaded her diapers, Mommy makes sure that she sits in them for a while before changing.

* * *

I am a baby boy in disposable diapers. I will be attending the open house with my lady friend/mommy on the second. We are both excited and very nervous. I am so excited to see the nursery. I hope you have cribs and other baby stuff. See you then.

* * *

I have visited and spent considerable time over the years being cloth diaper trained at various domination and fetish studios in the U.S. The cities include New York, Los Angeles, Boston and Chicago. All the doms at these studios were aware of my baby history.

The most memorable and outstanding was one in New York called (*he named it*). I believe the roster of doms was between fifteen and twenty. They were equipped with a baby nursery which featured a big baby crib, high chair, changing area and playpen. They were fully stocked with cloth diapers, disposable diapers, plastic panties, sleepwear for big babies, soothers, bottles, bibs, diaper pins and so forth.

Since there was a fine selection of stunning doms they were able to offer me young dominas who enjoyed playing the sexy, slim and youthful babysitter and were as relentless and mean as my sisters. Some of my favorite costumes of theirs were of course the private school girl outfits. But other times a sexy nurse's outfit was chosen or just faded Levis and a tight t-shirt. Every time I left the place I felt like a complete baby for hours afterwards due to the reality and professionalism the doms provided. At the end of each session the babysitter would invite other superior doms into the room to help humiliate me and restrain me while a large masseuse made me cum in my diaper. They really enjoyed this and so did I. They would look me straight in the eye and with great power stare at me like my sisters did.

In Los Angeles I went to an experienced dom who requested that I show up without diapers on and with a full bladder. Thus, on my arrival, I had no choice but to wet my trousers in front of the dom, who told me that diaper training would occur whether I liked it or not because like a helpless infant I couldn't control my bladder. The professional dom would then further embarrass me by calling over a young dom in training who loved to baby sit for naughty little boys. The head dom asked her assistant to drag me to the nursery for immediate diapering. It was the most exhilarating and humiliating thing I've ever experienced, because I wet myself in front of a dom in her early twenties and she happened to have a private school outfit on.

In Boston I saw a young professional dom who actually had a baby brother she often cared for when her mom couldn't. She enjoyed my sessions because my mannerisms and physicality reminded her of her baby brother. So the nanny scenario was played out.

I've also experience infantilism sessions in Chicago where they found my history fascinating and were equipped and willing to recreate it accurately. The studio in Chicago was always willing to play with me.

I look forward to my next experience with a passionate mommy and nannies played by professional doms at a fantasy play facility here in Toronto. Thank you for your kind attention.

*   *   *

Hi there. First, I must apologize for not responding sooner. I have wanted to respond for the longest time, I assure you. You may or may not remember me, so for reference our previous correspondence is pasted below this message.

It has taken me some time to dig deep and reflect on my thoughts and feelings and to more or less gain the courage as well as truly, fully express in words what kind of session I would really like.

To kick things off I will say that I do consider myself an adult baby. However, unlike many, I am not overly interested in a scenario in which I would receive maternal nurturing and perhaps delicate care. My key desires definitely lie deep in the world of being humiliated as a man forced back to babyhood completely against his will.

He tells me about himself, that he is successful, attractive and comes across as confident. Then he goes on, citing his previous correspondence.

In my fantasy I am shown my true self by a beautiful woman who sends me back to babyhood and makes the experience very unpleasant. This woman orders me to live out life as a baby in every respect possible with no return to adulthood in sight. I am forced into a diaper and my adult clothes are taken away. She humiliates me, taunts me and tells me the power she has over me. She openly teases me that she has done this to me and there is nothing I can do about it. She glories in her power over me. My hands are tied behind my back or I am kept in a straightjacket so I cannot do anything about it. I have to be fed and am not allowed to go to the toilet, but must make in my diaper, which she taunts me about. She displays me to other females who baby talk to me.

I hope it is possible to arrange this type of session.

*   *   *

To this very moment, there is absolutely and positively nothing to get me excited and aroused quite like the full babyfication treatment on the part of a head and superior professional dom (playing the part of mommy) and fully assisted by two younger professional dominas (playing the part of teenage babysitters or nannies).

By forcing me to regress back to a full baby state both physically and emotionally, principally through continuous diaper training, I feel completely free within the confines of a daycare center. I am thrilled when all three superior and powerful mistresses get full joy out of shaming me into soaking my thick and thirsty cloth diaper and plastic pants right before their eyes. Since I was an actual infant I knew no other way.

When I had just turned three years old my father left the house and never returned. My mother had difficulty dealing with his departure and began to travel a lot, leaving me in the hands of my two teenage sisters Irene (thirteen years my senior) and Susan (eleven years my senior).

Susan attended a local private girls' school. Irene used to study there too, however because she wasn't too scholastic minded she dropped out. Deep down inside she was very troubled by my father's sudden exit and blamed him and all other useless males for the inadequacies in the world. So Irene stayed home to "take care of me".

Like other children my age there was a potty handy in the bathroom, but mine was rarely used, because every time I had an accident Irene would enjoy punishing me with diaper training. So while all other kids were progressing with toilet training, I was regressing because of Irene's insistence in keeping me in thick cloth diapers and plastic panties.

All the neighbors assumed I was slower to develop and would eventually grow out of diapers, but this never happened. Nobody found out the truth about my sister's mischievous ploy to dominate me permanently, which is what she said most men deserved. As you can imagine, I was both frightened and continued wetting and messing my diaper, which was accompanied by complete babyfication and humiliation.

Irene would even encourage Susan and her private school friends to embarrass and shame me. Sometimes they would come in their school outfits and completely humiliate me with forced high chair feedings for hours on end. I can still hear their giggles as they called me "Baby Boy". I remember them forcing me to finish two or three bottles of apple juice as the pretty and slim teenage girls told me in their sexy and feminine voices that Babysitter Irene was waiting to prepare me for my nappy. Then they really enjoyed setting up for my diaper change.

I was now faced with these girls who chose to be mean to me. It seemed to give them great pleasure and a sense of power. They would poke and prod me and force me to wet my diaper until it began to drip and I was utterly soaked and uncomfortable. "All boys are babies" they would say as they held me down on my changing table and applied Vaseline, baby oil, diaper powder. They would also tickle me and pinch me while they held me down.

Then they would put me in my crib, raise the bars and restrain my limbs and force me to drink until I was full. They would turn the lights out and return hours later by which time, of course, I had wet myself again.

This routine continued for countless embarrassing years, with my mother knowing yet turning a blind eye. As I grew in years and size larger baby furniture and adult diapers and plastic pants were acquired. When the usual girls were unavailable other teenage girls came from the neighborhood to help my sisters restrain me while they did all this. They just assumed I was incontinent, and used a pacifier to silence me.

I have as a result never lived a normal life. To this day I am a full fledged adult baby and secretly wear cloth diapers every night. I look forward to being diaper trained by a professional dom and her younger dominatrices.

CHAPTER 7

Humiliate Me

As I have said before, there were certain things we would not do. But the clients certainly gave us a wide range of choices, and were generally not disappointed, in fact greatly impressed, when they found out, for real, that we would not perform sexual acts.

* * *

I am an experienced submissive. I have patronized mistresses in Amsterdam, New York, Paris, London, Los Angeles and Toronto.

Humiliation is the key. I need to be trained in how to serve and please as a submissive and slave. I should be required to beg to use the toilet, exhibited as a femme slave in front of women, be made to beg and whimper when being disciplined. Verbal humiliation is important. The mistress should criticize and mock me in front of other mistresses or women, particularly my appearance and how helpless I am when in bondage or how immobilized I am when cross-dressed in the manner I noted above. I should be made to worship my mistress and beg for punishment.

Please observe the color communication system: if the slave says yellow, limits are being reached, so please reduce or stop. If the slave says red, limits have been passed, so please stop and see what is bothering the slave. If slave says green, proceed. Please never leave the room or leave the slave alone when bound or locked up in any way.

Please avoid permanent marks: the paddle is for this reason the best form of corporal punishment—hard paddling after a suitable build-up. The slave should be taught how to take paddling in the most humiliating ways (on tip toe, in front of a mirror, giving thanks, having to choose which paddle or which body part is to be paddled, being made to count, being forced to stick out buttocks in a provocative, girlish posture before each stroke, not flinch, etc.).

Bondage should not be used extensively at the first session except for ankles (leg spreader or hobbling and thus forcing the slave to take baby steps) penis discipline and torment (for example, rope draped around the neck and then tied around base of penis and balls so that the slave cannot stand up straight without tightening the rope around the genitals and pulling the genitals up into a painful position: so the slave can be taught good posture). Perhaps in a later session, when the slave is familiar with the mistress fuller bondage can occur.

I like penis abuse within the limits of not causing damage. Make my balls sore and pinch the end of the penis. For example, use a pencil to tap one ball until it aches and slave has to beg to be hit on the other ball instead. Use standard techniques (constricting the base, etc.) to make my penis swell and get hard and to prevent ejaculation.

I have very tender and sensitive nipples. Manipulation of them makes me feel extremely submissive and aroused. Ice cubes, clothes pins, moderate clamps and even weights, if not too severe, are suitable.

My anus is very tender and has in the past been overused, overstretched and irritated. Please be very slow and tender in examinations, enemas, with dildos and so forth. It needs extensive and repeated lubrication.

I am also a cross-dresser. I like to be forced to walk in high heels, while wearing a garter belt, stockings, tight corsets and a tutu. Please avoid using facial makeup on me as I have allergies. Make me dance, prance and strut in front of mirrors.

*　　*　　*

My fantasy involves being your neighbor who has been caught stealing your panties from your clothesline, and you threaten to tell my wife unless I submit to your demands.

I first must strip for you to check if I'm not wearing any of your clothes. I then must stand naked in front of you and not move while you play with me, tease me and laugh at me, telling me how helpless I am at not being able to respond to your actions. You then order me on my knees to beg for forgiveness. As your humble and obedient toy, I would expect to be humiliated and degraded by you, a dominant woman, who enjoys forcing me to beg to worship your femininity. You would downgrade, taunt and tease my masculinity. You would talk down to me as if I was a little boy or girl and laugh at my helplessness and flaunt your sexuality.

While under your control, you would constantly touch and fondle me and tell me how much you enjoy seeing me so excited. Since I am so interested in women's clothing, you take me to your bedroom to show me your wardrobe and I am commanded to dress you in very feminine attire. But first, I must kneel before you or lie on the floor and worship your bare feet and tell you what an honor it is to be your foot slave. I might be ordered to kiss you all the way up your legs and between your legs. I might also be told to put my face between your thighs and be told to talk nicely and humbly to you.

You tell me that you would enjoy seeing me in women's clothing and you say you are going to teach me to be the perfect little lady. You then put me into a corset and stockings and high heels and order me to do your housework. You laugh as I struggle and then get impatient and angry. Finally you tell me to remove these garments. I can't reach the garters or get the corset off and you laugh and handcuff me and whip me while I am helpless. When you remove the handcuffs and the corset I kiss your feet and hands and thank you.

*   *   *

This mini-drama opens with a female boss sitting at her desk in an office. She is wearing a blue dress with oversized rim glasses. Her long hair is wept back tightly into a full pony tail permitting her to look both severe and feminine at the same time. She berates me in a heated but very professional tone of voice about my disrespectful and immature behavior towards her and other women. She gives me the options: being discharged from my job or submitting to a bare bottomed spanking over her lap.

I make a windy speech regarding the outrageous nature of this proposition but finally agree to punishment in order to save my job. She instructs me to take down my pants before her amused and watchful eyes. She leans over her desk revealing that she is not wearing any panties and extracts a black oval shaped hairbrush. Her eyes bright with mischief and power, she orders me across her knee and parts her thighs placing my prick between them. I submit willingly, hoping she will temper justice with mercy.

She brings the hairbrush down on my ass and I howl and try to roll off her lap, but she flexes her strong thigh muscles and keeps me in place. I soon lose control of my emotions and start sobbing, pleading and kicking. She keeps spanking me while I explode into an orgasm over her lap. I am so grateful for her clever spanking technique and her generous method of consolation that I drop to my knees and bury my face into her dark pubic patch.

* * *

I like my mistress to be cool and aloof during the session. She should be very dominant and demanding, hard to please and quick to punish. I enjoy both verbal and physical abuse, and desire my mistress to be very insulting about all my features. I like to be treated roughly during the session, pulled by the hair, slapped around, and generally treated with a very "hands on" type of domination.

I like my physical punishment to be either a spanking with a wide strap or paddle (no marks please) or a hard slap in the face with an open hand. I enjoy spankings while standing and leaning forward, with my mistress beside me. I also like the over the knee type stance. I prefer that the punishment be for offences during the session, rather than just being spanked for spanking's sake. I like the spankings to be quick and hard, say half a dozen hard, rapid spanks on each cheek, and then go on with something else. Likewise the slap in the face: sudden, without warning, hard enough to really sting and leave a red mark, and then go on. I do not want any restraints.

I wish to be made to worship your breasts and ass as much as permitted. I prefer the mistress to be in a standing position and to describe what she wants me to do in very crude language and intimate detail.

I enjoy being ridden horse style with the mistress holding my hair and whipping me just as a jockey would his mount, and digging in her high heels as spurs.

I would like my private parts punished by spanking and rough handling. Again, I prefer standing up and leaning back with legs apart, with my mistress in front with a strap or paddle. I enjoy a little pain here, so the strokes should slap fairly well. And don't forget a steady stream of dirty language. I would also like, if you have a small whip or stick, to be beaten on my bum.

* * *

I talked to you earlier and told you about my inability to lose the weight you wanted me to. I know I've disappointed you and deserve the caning you are going to give me.

You said it was going to be "harder than last time", so I guess you'll have to tie me down to the spanking box to restrain me. Last time you just bent me over and cuffed my hands and I was squirming around quite a bit while you spanked me. I even jumped off a couple of times. I know that when you really whip me I won't be able to stay still for it. Then again, I guess a good spanking should always be a little more than the culprit feels he can bear.

My last spanking left a few marks and bruises, so I'm sure this one will leave a lot of stripes, or maybe even draw some blood. I guess I deserve it. I was wondering if you could do one thing though. Please don't call me names or humiliate me as you punish me. It's humiliating enough just being naked and presenting my bottom for discipline without verbal abuse.

Treat me as if I were a wayward child, or a naughty schoolboy. Explain that you are sorry you have to punish me, but it is for my own good. Tell me what you are going to do before you begin, and let me know what I can expect if I continue to misbehave, but be compassionate.

I'm sorry I've disappointed you and I hope you'll give me another chance to show I can do better. I'll call soon to set up a time for you to spank me, cane me, or use your riding crop on me or whatever you feel is appropriate.

You may have noticed that right after he asked not to be verbally humiliated he proceeded to ask for it.

* * *

I'm interested in setting up a session with both [*he mentioned two of my staff*] to explore a fantasy I've had for about as long as I can remember. What I'm interested in is being smothered by having my face sat on full weight by a mistress playing the role of a boss figure, and a mistress playing the role of her assistant. Both parties remain fully clothed at all times, but the mistress uses her weight and smothering tactics to thoroughly defeat me. To intensify the situation the mistresses take pleasure in repeatedly passing gas while seated, having a sort of contest as it were. I feel really strange about contacting someone in regards to this, as I have absolutely no experience, just a fantasy. If this is the kind of scene you think might be allowed, please let me know and perhaps we can set up a time to meet. Thanks very much for your time.

*   *   *

I am looking for a lady to trample me all over my face, cock and balls, wherever your feet might land. I enjoy being used as a foot stool or a seat, but most of all as a rug. I like to be this for many women at once. I have a true passion for bare stockings or nylons on the feet without shoes but heels are fun too. If you are interested in seeing me please give me a shout.

*   *   *

I am an avid fetishist with special interests including: latex, boots, heels, gloves, hoods and some leather. Being fully outfitted in fetish gear is my favorite thing. The look, smell and feel of rubber provide me with intense pleasure.

My fantasy is to be dressed in latex and leather according to the directions and whims of a mistress. I enjoy being placed into various forms of bondage and teased, explored and dildo trained in various positions and degrees of helplessness.

I am a very visual fetishist, and love nothing more than to be in the company of a beautiful mistress dressed in full fetish attire while she uses me for her pleasure and satisfaction. The appearance of the mistress, and the surroundings, are very important to me.

I am not interested in extreme pain or humiliation, but am willing to explore my limits with the right person. I am not interested in extensive role playing or play acting. Otherwise I am looking for a creative mistress who enjoys what she does, and is able to provide me with some variety upon each visit.

I am looking to establish a lasting relationship with a mistress I can trust and have fun with. I have no medical conditions that prevent my participation in any of the activities I mentioned above. Hopefully this is the type of information that you require. I look forward to seeing your facility some time soon.

*   *   *

I wanted to write to you after checking out your wonderful Web site. I was impressed and frankly got a hard on just looking at it. I was fortunate enough to use your services back when you were still in Thornhill (before the manhunt began). You might not remember me. I was the guy who dressed as the Boy Wonder. I'm so happy to see you doing so well again and you facility pictures look stunning.

I hope you don't mind me being frank with you. I'm currently seeing a regular dom whose services I've been using for almost two years now on a fairly regular basis, but I'd love to maybe indulge myself once and try your amazing facility and one of your wonderful ladies. I would of course like to live out my favorite fantasy of being Robin the Boy Wonder finding himself in the clutches of an evil villainess. I have a major smoking habit and wonder if any of the ladies in your company are smokers. I also like the idea of your theme parties and if you ever have one that would allow a crime fighter like me to attend I'll be there.

I wish you continued success and if you have a moment sometime I would love to hear from you.

*   *   *

I saw your Web site. I'm very impressed by you and your mistresses, along with your facility. I called and was told to send an e-mail detailing my interest and an outline for a session. I know I'm not worthy to ask, but submit before you and beg that you might consider my request for a two day one night session. Below are some of my desires and an outline. I know the only desires that matter are yours, but I pray you might find me worthy.

I wish to be thickly diapered, the thicker the better, and dressed in little baby dolls or short skirts (maid, school girl or petticoat). I'm not a cross-dresser but I wish to be dressed this way as a form of humiliation.

90

I love all forms of humiliation and beg to serve as your sissy diaper maid or slave. I think serving as your sissy diaper "strap-on" slut would be very exciting.

*   *   *

This was from a client from 1994. There was no e-mail, so this was an actual letter and he gave his phone number. Many of his requests had to be refused, because of reasons I mentioned at the outset. We also did not have a male available for sessions like those he wanted.

After you receive this please hang on to it as I will be calling you for a price of an overnight stay. My holidays start in June for two weeks and any time during this period I can meet with you for a session. I am married and require secrecy from my wife and will in return obviously respect your wishes. If you wish to contact me I am home in the evenings at [*his phone number*].

Here is my fantasy. The biggest need in this session is to be humiliated, so if there is a time that I could be exposed to other people and be humiliated, go for it!

When I arrive you would have me strip naked and then tie me to the cross with my feet spread apart. Next you would apply bright red lipstick to my lips and then place a ball gag in my mouth to silence my pleas. After having done this you would place a full head cover on me which would deprive me of my sense of sight.

When you were happy with my situation, you could then begin my torture by placing nipple clamps on me and then starting some cock and ball torture or similar punishment. When this has been applied you could start the main part of my torture, which is to be teased and tormented without being allowed to cum. This could be done best by letting you work your own ways, and leaving the teasing up to you. Just about when it is time for me to be put down for the night you could have another (male) person begin to take advantage of me by fondling my penis and French kissing me on the mouth and just teasing me in general (not allowing me to cum). Some bright red nail polish could be applied to my finger and toe nails in preparation for the next morning. After this is done I could be securely tied down for the night in a position that does not allow me much movement and then have my mouth filled with a gag that is shaped as a penis (or the ball gag) and my butt filled with a large dildo that vibrates.

In the morning I would like to be made into a little slut frilly and put in full makeup and then dressed in a white corset and stockings. At this time I wish to be abused by a male person, being forced to take him in the ass and then to be forced to clean off his member with my mouth. At any time that the mistress or male person must use the washroom I wish to be the toilet. All through my session I wish to be teased, but never allowed to cum.

At the end of my session I would like to be tied in a manner that I have to suck my own cock and relieve myself and then made to swallow my own cum. I have heard that a person can be tied this way, but only if the mistress thinks that this is safe for me. If I cannot be tied this way I would like to have my feet pulled back over my head and then forced to relieve myself and swallow my own cum.

He then told me which other facilities he visited and what he did there. He had visited houses in the U.S. as well as Toronto.

I am able to attend a session on a Saturday night and sleep over Sunday and spend as much of the day Sunday as needed. I am married and need to be very discreet, with no visible signs left on my body.

He did come for some sessions and understood that most of what he requested was off the table. I was raided a few months after he sent that first letter. He was obviously a very successful man. He drove a luxury car and he had the appearance and bearing of a senior executive.

CHAPTER 8

Torture Me

The clients were of course advised that we could bind and torture their genitals but that we were not permitted to bring them to orgasm. This was our understanding of the law. The law permitted punishment but not pleasure. I was never raided or charged in Toronto like I was in Thornhill, which borders on Toronto, despite the fact that the two operations did not differ on what was and what was not done. I have already spoken before about the things we would not do, but let me say again I am just sharing their fantasies with you as they requested them in writing.

* * *

As you aware, I am reporting to you for correction. I thought I would use this note to familiarize you with my needs. Unlike many of your clients, I get very little sexual gratification from being punished. I find that I lack self-discipline, and occasionally I need a good bare bottom spanking to set me on the straight and narrow.

I am coming to see you because I promised myself that I would lose twenty pounds before Christmas, and I am failing miserably. While I dread the thought of having my bottom caned, I know that I am richly deserving of punishment. I would not be so presumptuous as to tell you how you might administer correction, but generally I think a spanking should be severe enough that the culprit will remember it each time he sits down for the next few days. Of course a good caning will leave a lot of marks on the behind and the tops of the thighs, and if the cane happens to cut the bottom, it is only to be expected.

As the chastiser, you alone will determine the length and severity of my punishment and should pay little heed to my pleas for mercy. A sound thrashing will obviously be more than I feel I can bear, and once you have me in position, you should gauge my punishment by the condition of my bottom, not by what I think I deserve.

You should place me in whatever position you find is best suited for caning a naughty bottom, and use whatever restraints you feel are necessary to keep me in position. A cane is the instrument I am usually punished with, since I think it imparts the maximum pain with each stroke, and leaves stripes on the offending bottom to remind the culprit of the consequences of misbehaving. However, if you have some other instrument that you prefer to use, please feel free. Just remember that the goal is maximum deterrent value.

Finally, since the aim of the punishment is behavior modification, you should use your opportunity to drive home your message by reminding me why I'm here. Statements like "I'm sorry I have to do this . . ." or "This is going to hurt me more than it hurts you . . . ." are what I am looking for. You might also comment on the condition of my bottom as the punishment progresses, and tell me what I can expect from you if I continue to miss my weight loss goals. You might tell me that you will give me a certain type of punishment if I fail to lose five pounds by December first. You could say "I used a riding crop on a young woman's behind last week because she cheated on her husband. I fastened her over the edge of a desk and flailed away at her ass cheeks until I drew blood. That's what you can expect if you don't lose the weight I order you to lose."

I am sure someone as experienced as you at discipline doesn't need to hear anything more from me. I have been naughty and deserve to be spanked. I leave the rest in your hands. Rest assured that as I stand before you I am afraid of what you are about to do. But I am also sure that after you are finished I will be tearful, contrite and grateful for putting me in line again.

*   *   *

The object of the session is to continually stimulate my balls. The session will end with a slow, torturing masturbation. The session is to be at a medium level. After I undress the Mistress attaches my hands to a collar ring and leaves. A female submissive takes me to a shower, stimulates my cock and balls with soap and oral stimulation (if permitted). She covers my genitals with warm oil and leaves.

The Mistress attaches an elastic band around my balls to ensure they remain vulnerable for stimulation, and should be continually grasped, rubbed, held and teased. The elastic may be replaced with a similar leather device which produces a similar effect—vulnerability. She attaches a leash to the band, gags me, and puts me on a bondage table and my feet into a spreader bar. She frequently grabs my balls for teasing.

The Mistress removes the spreader bar and takes me off the table. She leads me through the halls on a leash, stopping occasionally so a female submissive can grasp my balls. If other females are around they may be asked to hold my balls and kiss me passionately. The Mistress then attaches me to a bondage device, where I am left standing with the spreader bar reapplied, and leaves me for fifteen minutes.

A female submissive comes in and tortures my balls alternately with ice cubes and a warm cloth. She occasionally grabs my balls and reminds me of my helplessness. She may kiss me occasionally and stimulate my cock with a feather, but not too much. She tickles me all over with the feather, and then tickles my balls mercilessly.

The Mistress then comes in and ties the female submissive to the bondage table, tickles her mercilessly with a feather and then masturbates her to orgasm. She then releases the sub and ties me to the bondage table and leaves.

When she returns she tortures me with the feather and teases my genitals and then slowly masturbates me to orgasm.

*   *   *

Here are two very similar scenarios from different individuals, both referring to both the good and evil females in secret agent movies.

Unwittingly I have become aware of secret information which requires my liquidation. I have been discovered and am about to be interrogated and tortured by a beautiful, seductive, but cruel woman. This woman is the specialist for the "company" because she enjoys her work, obtaining sadistic sexual pleasure from toying with her victims before killing them, like a cat with a mouse.

For half of the session the woman is wearing a black satin dress (leather is okay) and underneath it a black satin corset, sheer nylon stockings and black stiletto heels. For the second half she removes the dress. For authenticity there is pain. Feel free to test my limits. My erection will tell you all you need to know. For the most part though, I am aroused more by suggestion of the unthinkable, rather than actual pain. I am excited by the image of a beautiful woman who drives sexual pleasure from inflicting pain and worse, and hearing of the fate of your other helpless victims would be a powerful stimulant. I am very tactile, and love the feel of satin, soft leather, and nylon against my genitals and the rest of my body. Long satin gloves are a particular turn-on.

I like restraints, particularly suspension. However the restraints should not be too uncomfortable, as this is a distraction. I like being stroked and beaten with a whip. I like pain being inflicted by stiletto heels. I like forced oral sex. I like the threat of cigarette torture. I like being penetrated by a woman wearing a strap-on dildo.

I do not like golden showers, severe cock and ball torture or humiliation. It just doesn't turn me on.

*　　*　　*

You are evil international terrorists. I am a female government agent you have abducted with the purpose of torturing for information that will assist you in some kind of terrorist act. After you are satisfied with the information that you have gained from me, you will torture me further out of hatred and finally you will attempt to kill me by way of some diabolical deathtrap. Being exposed to the exterior elements is also a possibility. It is important that the role play appears to be realistic.

You may use the forms of suspension I described on the questionnaire, which are numerous. If I can endure the pain, you may place the candles that I have provided for you beneath my feet. I would also like to be stretched on "the rack" and have a space heater exposed to my feet. Drip hot candle wax on my stomach. Beat the soles of my feet with a leather strap. Light face slapping for realism is permitted. Moderate whipping is allowed. I really like having my bonds gradually tightened so that they cut off both my air and blood circulation. You may also tie me up outside to a pole or tree if possible. I like to be tied up in ladies' clothing both fully dressed and in my undergarments and hosiery. However, fell free to remove any article of my clothing whenever it gives you pleasure or enhances the realism of the role play. I prefer to be tied with rope, especially by my ankles and legs. Spreader bars are also a possibility. You may gag me but I prefer a bit gag. Blindfolds are permitted but only when I am being abducted or prepared for torture, not during.

You are not to remove my bra, underwear or hosiery. You must not damage any of my clothing or allow stains or tears on it. I do not like hoods, collars or caning. Anything that might cause me to bleed is forbidden. I am not into any form of extreme sexual humiliation such as golden showers or dildos.

*   *   *

I would like to have my wrists and ankles bound and be forced to crawl on the floor. I would also like you to be sadistic-like and say "Does it hurt? Good, I like you to suffer." Lashing me on my sun burned back you say "My, that must hurt! Good. Suffer. Now crawl on your belly." You should also step on me periodically and grab my hair and yank me around.

I'm not crazy about the nipple clamps and I don't need to masturbate, but do enjoy a caress on my penis, even with your shoes or feet. Please eliminate saying "Please do another Mistress", and keep striking unless I say "red" (if I am in restraints or tied).

*   *   *

One of my goals in this adventure is to stop smoking. Please allow me no more than three cigarettes the first day and none the second day. Bondage is my fetish. When you put me in the prison cell have me tied up hand and foot. I like the straight jacket for the nights. To feel truly powerless please have me wear the cock harness attached by a leash held in my mistress's hand when changing positions. To maximize the intensity of this experience, I would appreciate permission to smoke three to five joints. I would like to wear a hood at all times if possible. For meals, I am allergic to mayonnaise and mustard.

*   *   *

97

I have been sent for correctional therapy due to a bad attitude towards women. You decide that the remedy is for me to become a woman permanently, so as to be pretty and vulnerable and be taken for (and fucked) as a woman. Initially I refuse, but after periods of torture and bondage, including strict interrogation, I eventually agree and admit that this is what I want.

For bondage I prefer ropes. I want to be tied into a leather corset, perhaps with a hood, blindfold and/or gag. I am to be tortured until I agree to feminization. You are not convinced, and I am returned to a cell each time this happens. You change outfits each time I am in the cell to demonstrate how to become pretty. The torture and interrogation should be with a strap and by sitting on my face.

I am to be cross-dressed fully: clothes, hair, makeup, nails, jewellery and perfume. Then I am to be tied up again and put into the cell with a mirror in front. I want you to be strict, unbending and never friendly. Initially you wear a dominatrix outfit, but then change to pretty feminine outfits to demonstrate what will happen to me. It is important that you say things like "You are a ridiculous, pathetic male and must become my female slave—permanently." The rest is up to you.

* * *

Your Web site is just terrific. It is the best free one I have seen. If you would be so kind as to e-mail back to me what form of punishment I can expect to look forward to on Monday it would give me something to dream about. Your water torture, soap and Tabasco sauce torture sound exciting, as does prolonged interrogation. Whatever you decide, if you could give me a little peek of what is in store I could think about it over the weekend and dream about my visit.

* * *

Wonderful site! I plan to be in Toronto within the next few weeks and was hoping to get more information regarding a session. Please let me know which of your lovely ladies would be most adept at inflicting cruel tickle torture, especially foot tickle torture. I would love to have a tickling session, and also a foot fetish session (therefore a mistress with gorgeous feet too). Any recommendations? I am not interested in any other forms of BDSM (humiliation, spankings, infantilism, etc.), just foot fetishism and tickling.

Ideally, if one of your ladies happens to be a switch (or would be willing to switch for this scene), I would love to be able to inflict a little "revenge tickling" as well, as part of a scenario.

* * *

I saw you on television back in October and was floored by your statement that "Tickle torture is my stock in trade." I would love information on pricing and bookings. I work banker's hours so evenings and weekends are best for me. I am looking for about an hour and am interesting in knowing as well what kinds of equipment you have to immobilize me for tickling. What kind of lovely instruments of tickle torture do you have at your disposal? What is your policy on genital tickling? What clothing would I wear during tickle torture? I love verbal admonishment and teasing from my torturer.

* * *

Mistress, at your request, and if it would please you, I would like to give you a scenario that would be of great pleasure to me.

I like to be tied tightly so as not able to move, and be gagged with your panties. Then I am to be pinched and teased relentlessly as you whisper how helpless I am. You look at me with your entrancing eyes and prolong my agony, which is very erotic and sensual. You tie up my penis and scrotum and rub the head of my penis with the palm of your hand and hot wax to make me squirm and confess my desire for you.

* * *

At my Thornhill house, Madame de Sade's House of Erotica, the advertising and layout of the house conveyed more of an S&M emphasis, as opposed to sissy maid training, although cross-dressing was still very popular with clients. This client wrote out a number of very extreme scenarios, most of which I had to refuse. They involved penetration and too much handling of genitals. We had to assume all clients were police officers. I was known as Mistress Marie to most clients. Here is one of six scenarios of his I have on hand, which I could only partially agree to.

From a standing position Mistress Marie will mummify my body by wrapping me completely with Saran Wrap, tape and rope, exposing only my nipples, ass, cock and balls for her unrestricted pleasures. My arms will be wrapped tightly against my sides and my legs and feet will be secured firmly together underneath me. Upon completing the mummification Mistress Marie will secure me to a bondage table so that she may access my nipples, asshole and cock and balls. Further bondage apparatus such as clamps will be attached to my nipples. Dildo training will begin with a variety of butt plugs and dildos being shoved up my ass and held securely in place with harnesses or wrap. Finally, my cock and balls will be locked up with special harnesses, straps, rings and rope and left weighted to tug forever on my cock and balls. I do not mind being hooded but I do not want my eyes covered so that I may see what is going on as Mistress Marie is a very visual turn-on for me.

CHAPTER 9

Cook Me

This extraordinary fantasy was given to me at my Thornhill house. The police showed it to each other during the raid and considered using it as evidence at my trial. I did not do the car capture part, or of course use all the ingredients mentioned.

*   *   *

I am playing a little boy walking down the street. You drive up to me, stop, get out and put me into your car trunk and slam it shut. When you get to your house you take me down to the dungeon and lock me in a cell. In a few minutes you bring me cookies and water, which I eat. After I have eaten the cookies you tell me that they are made from little boys and describe in detail the preparations involved (describing in general what I will write below).

You change and bring me upstairs to show me tapes of previous meals, following which you take me to the kitchen, tear my shirt off and tie my hands. You sit on my chest and take my pants off, leaving only my underwear. You probe and pinch and weigh, checking for proportions.

You then put me back in the cell. You moon me as you leave. The phone rings. Your ghoulish neighbor saw you bring me in. She also loves to eat boys. Here is what I hear you saying over the phone.

"Hello. (Pause) Oh hi. (Pause) Just fine, how about you? (Pause) Oh, you saw him come in! Ha, ha. Of course I'm going to eat him. Don't I always? (Pause) You always have a standing invitation. (Pause) I'll probably BBQ him tomorrow night. I have another guest coming, so he's a bit small. (Pause) Well, he's eighty-three pounds, but for three hungry women you need ninety. (Pause) Yeah, there are a lot of waste bones and guts and so on. (Pause) I thought I'd start with garden salad. (Pause) I find the salad helps the meal go down easier. (Pause) If you wish to, yes, potato salad would go nice with him. (Pause) A big bowl is fine. Perfect. (Pause) No, I have everything else. I have lots of beer. (Pause) That's great. Just bring the potato salad and a big appetite. Come early so we can have cocktails before dinner."

You make a second call and invite [*he gives the name*], my former dom. She'd love a portion. I listen in horror in the dark to the conversation. Ad lib the conversation.

You come for me wearing only an apron, heels, bra and panties. You pull me out and prod me up the stairs, mocking me on the way to the kitchen. You have me sit and let me take one last long look at the outside world as you read the recipe and check ingredients out loud. You tease me with your panties as you do so.

"For the Mediterranean head cheese the head is boiled and fermented with spice to make about ten kilograms of cheese. The neck will be scrap meat for my dogs. I'll follow a Russian recipe for the organs: pickled liver, kidneys and heart. All other internal organs will also be used as pet food. I'll follow a Persian recipe and use the chest and back meat for ground meat loaf—baked slowly and spiced. I'll follow the Montana BBQ recipe for the buttocks: rump roast, sliced off in one piece, sent to age and then roasted. I'll follow the Greek recipe for the legs—stripping off all meat and marinating it. So let's see. I'll need one boy weighing ninety to one hundred pounds, one red onion, one garlic clove, one liter of olive oil, one pepper, five hundred milliliters of Worcester sauce, two hundred grams of salt, ten pounds of rice for optional stuffing, one liter of hot BBQ sauce and one apple for the boy's mouth to keep him quiet. I roast him on the spit three minutes for each pound he weighs to cook rare and four minutes per pound for medium. I keep rotating and brush regularly."

You then come to the cell and take me away. I beg and plead. I kiss your feet and legs (if that is o.k.) and get dragged to the BBQ pit (table). On the way you have me stop in the bathroom for one last time. You drag me out and once at the BBQ I run for the door. You come for me slowly and push me slowly with your body back to the table. You lie me down on the table next to the BBQ, tie my feet and hands and blindfold me. You oil me (with baby oil), season me (with talcum powder), and wrap parts of me in Saran Wrap.

Then you brush the sauce (water) on as you munch chips and drink beer. I beg for a beer. You laugh and tell me that soon I'll be swimming in beer. You put an apple in my mouth and put your panties on a pillow and then near my nose and cover my face with them.

I hear muffled voices. You make jokes with the other ladies and so forth. Anyway, we can discuss the ending.

CHAPTER 10

Mistress Doctor

Medical fetishes are common, no doubt because of early life trauma in the form of visits to the doctor. The powerful nurse remains fixed in the mind.

* * *

I visit the doctor for a complete physical. The nurse takes me to a room and asks me to undress to my underpants with her present. She explains she has seen lots of men, and asks the routine questions as I am undressing. Then she weighs me and takes my height and waist measurements. She discovers I have wet my underpants. She points this out and treats me like a small child who has been bad. The doctor, a woman, comes in and the nurse shows the doctor what I have done. The doctor orders me to be bathed and dressed in training panties and a nightgown. If the nurse is not pleased with my behavior I'm to be given a spanking on the bare bum. However, I am usually in panties or underpants.

* * *

Please allow me to introduce myself. I am a fifty-five year old single, unattractive accountant on the outside, but on the inside I am a desirable twenty-two year old woman. I have trouble approaching women; they tend to ignore me when they see me coming so I avoid socializing with them altogether. I tremble with fear just being in their company. The women I work with are untouchables. They don't even know or care that I exist. I am still a virgin. I have been tempted to see a prostitute but my conscience won't go for it. Too scared to try, I go limp just thinking about having to perform sexual intercourse on a woman. Because of my inability to communicate with women or my defect in character I have resigned my quest for marriage and now dedicate my life to taking care of my elderly mother. My mother is overbearing, dominant and argumentative. As a young boy she dressed me like a girl until I was nine years old. I was always teased at school by the bully girls, and I ran home in tears almost every day.

I am asexual and have no desire for sexual intimacy; however I do have a fixation for my family doctor. I fantasize she is giving me a physical examination, but I am a girl. Over the past year I have become a hypochondriac. I go on the Internet and look for symptoms that I might mimic in order to have her touch me in certain areas of my body. It feels so good when she lays her hands on my body and asks me if it hurts. She smells like medicine. She wears white latex gloves while she pokes, prods and caresses my vulnerable body parts. I feel alive when she pays me attention. She is soft and gentle with me in person but in my fantasy she is a cruel evil scientist and I am her guinea pig lab rat captured in her laboratory dungeon.

Over the past month I have made three appointments for an examination, I think she's caught on that I have a fetish for her and I'm afraid she may ask me to find another doctor. I need help. Could you please help me? I can't take it any longer. It's driving me insane. I am masturbating three or four times a day, a bad habit that's out of control.

I would like to live out my fantasy at your house for a day. Can you provide me with a professional dominatrix that would act like my doctor and teach me to control my excitement? I would like a complete physical examination by a mistress in white latex uniform cap and gloves. I would like her to be cruel and uncaring. I would like her to scream orders at me to turn around and bend over to examine and inspect my buttocks. I would like her to make derogatory remarks about my body parts and how they will be surgically removed. I would like to be prepped for a sex change operation by several cruel heavy set nurses. I would like be given several invasive medical tests. Blindfold me and stick me with pins as if I were getting multiple needle injections. Two nurses administer an enema while discussing my diagnosis amongst them. Prepare me for surgery. Shave my balls and ass. Hot wax my balls so they are completely covered, and then freeze my balls with crushed ice. Insert breast implants and my sex change operation is complete.

Thank you so much for considering my request.

*   *   *

I report for my check-up. I am led to the examination room in your basement by the receptionist. She tells me to take my clothes off and have shower and lie down on the table. I do this. Then a mistress dressed as a nurse comes in and tells me that I must be restrained for the examination. She straps me to the table spread eagled, speaking encouraging words to me. When she is finished she starts to laugh and ties my cock. Then she puts a ball in mouth gag on me. She then puts baby powder all over me and tickles me mercilessly. When she has done this for several minutes she leaves. Another mistress in a lab coat comes in and looks at me with disgust. She tells me she is Doctor (You make up a name) and she will examine me. She does some tapping and listening with a stethoscope. Then she begins pinching me, attaches nipple clamps and all the while orders me to stop squirming and crying out because it is making her angry. She becomes more and more cruel. Then she gets a whip and administers it to my stomach, chest and legs and the bottoms of my feet. She is relentless and appears to get more aroused the more I suffer. When she has done this for several minutes she lightly whips my balls. Then she calls for the nurse and tells her the examination is complete and the patient can go home. The doctor leaves and closes the door. The nurse is smiling and laughs and says the doctor is gone now and I am completely at her mercy. She tickles and pinches me for a prolonged period, constantly laughing and asking me if I want more, yet not stopping when I shake my head. When my time is up she finally releases me. I would like to shower before leaving.

CHAPTER 11

Let Me Worship You

You may have seen pictures of me in the media sitting on a "throne" in full leather, perhaps holding a riding crop. Worship means men prostrating themselves in front of such a queen or goddess and perhaps kissing her boots or feet and telling her how they feel about her. But, as you will see in the final letter in this chapter, it may also take the form of worshipping a media image.

*   *   *

I am a twenty-three year old slave in Toronto. My biggest fetish is foot domination and foot worship. I would like to know if I can arrange to worship at your feet. Please tell me your rates and hours.

*   *   *

I wanted some information on the services you can provide that don't involve sissy maid training or classes, or feminization programs, since I have no interest in these things. I am a very passive guy. I'm fifty-four and do clerical work in an office.

I absolutely adore you and think you truly are a superior, exalted goddess. I wanted to know if you are permitted currently to allow clients to engage in basic humiliation and groveling. What I basically want is to body-worship a brutal, nasty, arrogant, divine supreme being who craves and demands the following from subordinates or slaves: profound foot-worship, intense ass adoration, service as a chair, floor mat or pony. She enjoys verbally degrading these human lackeys. I don't wish any extreme activities and I don't need to be undressed. I simply wish to kneel at your feet while you are reclining, resting with your powerful, god-like feet thrust into my face for worship and adoration. I have a million fantasies like that, yet I am still a novice and just beginning to realize them in actual life. Are you permitted to do these things? I have passed over your ads because I have no interest in the sissy training and so forth, like I said earlier. If you are able to do these milder activities with virtually no props required I would love to try it. I apologize for the length of this letter.

*   *   *

I hope I can refresh your memory about me. I was at your school a little over a month ago for a half day sissy maid session. I had confused the time a bit and I had to leave before the whole time was used. Thanks to your kindness I returned a few weeks after to finish my remaining hour, and you took me downstairs. Both times at your school were awesome experiences. Thank you again! I would like very much to visit with you again. You suggested that I e-mail you and discuss some possible scenarios to play out. Let me tell you what I enjoyed. I'm sure that with your experience you will be able to tell what is best for me.

It really excited me to be dressed up by you. The maid's outfit was fantastic. I loved the feeling. I felt so sexy and feminine. The makeup was incredible. You made me really look like a girl as well. Dressing like that and feeling like that and having you instruct me in walking, curtsying and sitting was so very exciting. I really liked the walking, curtsying and sitting lessons. I think that I would enjoy lessons like that again, and kneeling and talking lessons too. The makeup lessons would not really benefit me—as I do not dress outside of your school. I don't plan to. I see your school as a getaway of sorts, something to enjoy every now and again when I am able. That's why lessons in domestic servitude really wouldn't sit well with me. I'm not going to actually go out and become a sissy maid.

As far as the basement (dungeon), that was something brand new for me also—and just as exciting. I didn't care too much for the painful nipple attention, but everything else when I was restrained on the table was very exciting. Being bound is very interesting and exciting. I do trust you. What really excited me was when you first had me stripped on the floor and you came into the room and sat on your swing and had me kiss and massage your feet. There was something incredibly sexual, I didn't know exactly what I could do, but I'm sure next time I will really kiss and suck and lick your feet and toes (if it will please you). I apologize if I am being long winded. I look forward to worshipping you.

*　*　*

In 2012 a gentleman wrote to me. I will call him Mr. Gloves. He was following my recent case in the media. We have never met. Here is what he said and what happened.

I'm fifty-nine and have followed your case and seen your image on various news vehicles. I've tried in vain to contact you in the past to no avail. I'm not sure if this will get to you but I want to say that I'd love to meet you. I've known I was masochistic since I was a wee boy as well as in love with leather gloves, leather heels and ballet slippers. I know articles say you are retired but I wish I could contact you. Please make my dream come true and e-mail me back. When I saw your leather encased hands in the newspaper I melted. Please write to me so we can communicate.

I wrote back and told him I was flattered.

I can't believe I'm actually hearing back from you. It's indeed an honor and at the same time a wee bit intimidating, to be honest with you. I've never ever in my whole life been brave enough to act on my impulses or talk to anyone about my wants and desires, strange as they may be; but with you dressed in leather and always with your fabulous gloves on I really am attracted to you. You have probably encountered guys very similar to me. I live in Oakville and for some reason I think you are a west end lady or maybe Toronto. The closest I've ever come to living out my dreams and desires is by finding abandoned ladies' leather gloves and coveting them.

I'd love to hear back from you. Could you let me know more about a possible meeting? Is there anything more you want to know more about me? Honestly I'm actually nervous right now but at the same time I'm fifty-nine and never acted on these impulses. It's perhaps about time! Is there anything you could suggest to ease my stress level or that would facilitate me being more brave about this? I'd certainly be eager to attain the gloves that have graced your hands. Would this honor be attainable? Let me know.

I would be into anything you might suggest. Please lay some ground rules. I want to really trust you and would love it if you could and would trust me. You are indeed fascinating and when you rest up from your busy, busy schedule I'd be so honored to hear back from you.

To actually hear back from you already has been a terrific honor. I hope I haven't offended you in any way. I'd love to be a slave to you and your black leather sensuous gloves. If we had tea, would you wear your gloves for me? Thanks for your kind words, they mean a lot to me! In due course and when you get rested up, would you write to me again? I'd love to hear back from you about what I've suggested and about yourself. You're so fascinating and goddess like!

First and foremost, Take care of yourself.

P.S: With all my heart I covet your gloves. If I had a pair of your well worn ones I'd have died and gone to heaven!

I wrote back and told him I was retired but that I appreciated his kind words. Then he wrote to me again.

I'm hoping that this e-mail will not disturb you from your resting up time. I promised myself not to bother you but I thought that as your gloves, the ones that you wore recently in the *Sun* holding your riding crop and showing the victory sign were so very attractive to me, they are driving me crazy, just staring at them in the paper, I thought that I would ask you outright if I could somehow acquire them. Please let me know. As I say, I hate to pester you, but they have become a wee bit of an obsession with me.

It would mean the world to me to have your gloves, ones that you've worn with your wonderful and natural scent on them. I admire you so, so very much and with my leather glove fetish this would be heaven on earth to me! Please let me know if this is achievable. I would respect them and never soil or dirty them and only treat them pristinely and reverently. I would hold them on a pedestal just as I do you!

I know you would know how much they would mean to me. Please my Mistress/Goddess would you in all your thoughtfulness, let me know if this is possible? In any event I'd love to hear back from you. If you like be brutally honest with me. I'm extremely happy just to have heard back from you in the first place, from a Canadian icon and leather bound beauty!

Sorry to harp on this subject and to bother you again, but what I had planned to do (I'm not sure whether this qualifies for "fortune taking a turn", but I hope so) was to pay up front for a new pair of gloves if you know what the costing would be. When you purchase the new gloves, and only then, you would send me the ones that you are wearing now in the mail. Is that o.k.? That way you wouldn't be gloveless at all and you'd be getting a brand new pair of equivalent gloves or even better ones if possible. Please tell me that this would be o.k. You could also charge me extra if you like (lets call it for a "wearing fee") as for me your gloves are priceless. Please say yes. I'm desperate for your gloves and you won't be out at all and you'd be getting a new pair.

The only extra hardship to you would be to go and get a new pair which would be an inconvenience for a busy lady like yourself, I do realize that but you'd be gaining a new pair of gloves and you'd be making a devoted fan of yours the happiest man in the universe. I swear! You wouldn't be out any money. In fact you would be getting the extra wearing fee (your "fortune taking a turn").

I wrote and told him a supporter would arrange to meet with him and sell him my gloves and give him a specially inscribed copy of my book.

Yippee! What an Easter, in fact an all occasion, surprise! Thanks from the bottom of my heart!

I'm not a rich man, Terri-Jean, but this is very meaningful to me. Thanks for the opportunity. By the way it would be important for me to know the size of your gloves. They are meaningful for me just to have them, something of yours that you've worn with your natural scent on them but if I could actually put them on my own hands this would be extra special for me to just to imagine to myself that you were wearing them. You probably understand.

I was so excited to get your reply I couldn't sleep last night. Remember I did tell you I was a little nervous and reticent about certain things like grabbing the bull by the horns and living out my dreams. As such I'm a little nervous about meeting your key supporter and yes, even you.

However I somehow have trust in you and would be prepared to meet with your key supporter, to exchange money for the gloves and to hear what he has to say from there. I'd be honored to receive your book.

My supporter met him. They had a nice lunch. He bought the gloves. Naturally I was very curious to know what he was like. My supporter told me he was a very conservative looking and well spoken professional man. He had a family and said he never acted on his masochistic or fetish impulses. He said that perhaps at some time he would be in touch and would be very pleased to meet me. He wrote to me a few days later and said no words could describe how happy he was with the gloves.

CHAPTER 12

Take My Slave

It is likely that some of these were written by the clients themselves as part of their fantasy of having one woman giving him to another for punishment or training. In some cases the letters were from actual mistresses, again catering to the client's fantasy in this regard. Finally, some actually were from wives or girlfriends sending their partner to me. Of these, some may yet again be catering to the man's fantasy, but I know for a fact that a few were genuinely from women who are actually catering to their own desires.

* * *

I am delivering this excuse for a slave into your expert hands in the hope that you can teach him his station in life and how to properly serve and service his mistress.

This morning he walked in on my girlfriend and me as we were enjoying each other. He had the audacity to try and join in to satisfy his own desires. Do these slaves not realize that they exist only to please us in the fashion we desire? Clearly he should be punished for this sort of behavior and then shown the way to respond to his mistress's wishes and please her body on a prolonged basis.

You should conduct a thorough examination to see that he has the necessary equipment and nothing is concealed. He responds well to discipline sessions, including cock and ball restraint and spanking paddles. To get his full attention I have found that cock and ball torture works the best, rewarded with the occasional release. Then he must be trained to worship his mistress as she so desires.

Of course any other ideas you might have will be greatly appreciated. He is in your hands. I hope he returns more appreciative of our desires and ready to serve as commanded.

* * *

I found your Web address online, and looked through the items it contained. I found much of the information interesting, and having been to other BDSM bed and breakfasts in the past wanted to find out more information about what your facility offered. I have my own slave, and have not found it necessary to involve others in his training as of yet.

Please send me either an e-mail or a Web address that contains more detailed information if it is available. From the information provided on your Web page I believe that a private suite is what I would be most interested in. I also am interested in knowing what your guidelines as far as smoking and alcohol are. In the past I have been limited with activities including fire play, so I would also be interested in your policy regarding this activity. Thank you for your time and assistance. I am, Lady S.

* * *

This letter was sent by another Mistress to whom I sent this sissy. The sissy was made to thank me on his knees for sending him and then was whipped for not getting better grades on the performance of his duties.

The following tasks were performed today by this sissy: vacuuming living room and stairs (good), cleaning table tops (good), vacuuming back guest room (not good), washing mirrors in the living room (excellent), cutting vegetables for lunch salad (good) and cleaning up after lunch (good).

She stood politely at attention with her eyes lowered when not occupied by her job. She removed her high heels without permission. The scones she made were lovely, light and fresh. I would love to have her on a regular basis Mondays.

* * *

I am a woman and have been with my girlfriend, who is five years older than me, for almost three years. We wish to try something to maintain and improve our relationship. We are from Hong Kong where we are professional level employees. We are rather open-minded. My girlfriend is my boss. She loves me very much and at home I am her mistress in all respects. She begs me to tie her up, beat her and make me her slave in all respects. I enjoy being dominant, but don't know what to do for our mutual pleasure.

We came across your site and believe you can assist us. We will be vacationing on the east coast of North America in a few months and will be spending time in the Toronto area. Should I go to see you alone at first and you get someone to play my girlfriend, or should we both come? I want to learn how to make her a slave. Let us know how to contact you when we are in Toronto. She also wishes to know generally what you are prepared to do to her if she comes too. At the moment I only beat her slightly, give her a little nipple torture and make her kneel at my feet kissing my toes and worship me and beg for punishment. She apparently wants more, but as she is small I really don't know what else I can do to her.

* * *

Our maid behaved quite well today. She took it upon herself to anticipate my needs on more than one occasion. Every task I set out for her was performed to the best of her ability. Towards the end of her cleaning duties, she gave me a massage. It was quite acceptable. My suggestion to you is to work with her on her curtsey. It is not that she forgets, but that she lacks grace and style.

* * *

I have given your address to my personal "girl" [*she gave "her" name*] and instructed her to attend your next party. Did she contact you? This is a word of recommendation. She is quite well trained. I am a lifestyle dom in New York and I use her often for demos of pony work or bondage and hard punishment or when I go to my girlfriends' parties, or other dungeons. Then I lay it on! I sometimes use a blindfold to confuse her.

I saw your Web site and would like to get up there some time. She needs to lose a bit of belly but apart from that I've been pleased for the last four years. I lend her out to friends. It turns me on when she returns with marks that last a long time. She needs to be kept in training. I also demand that she is always shaved and ready to dress up as a college girl. She gets so embarrassed. I have instructed her to wear her chain at all times. Please feel free to call me. Use her as you like.

* * *

You have seen [*"her" name is given*] before, about a year ago. Could she please be taken on the tour and given a good bare bottom spanking with as many people watching as possible. She is wearing garters, panties and nylons and her t-shirt is quite long and is like a dress. Could she please go on the tour without her boy pants and t-shirt on?

Here is the money. She has an equal amount on her if you wish to put a maid's outfit on her and give her some lessons. I will leave that up to you, but if she does stay for the extra time it should only be if others will be seeing her humiliated. She also has some questions to ask you about her last lesson. She has just had her bottom waxed smooth, which was very humiliating for her.

* * *

Thank you very much for your thoughtful note. I am sending this slave with several toys you may find useful in teaching him to be a good student. I'm sure you understand my strategy. I want him to be knocked off balance from his familiar thinking and automatic male behavior, so that a more docile and submissive mindset can be quickly installed. He is a typical male: sloppy and careless of details. Your academy and ideas should provide him with plenty of strict discipline and punishment for his misdeeds, and hopefully put him on a new course quickly. He is certainly good submissive material, but the road to the goal might be bumpy at times and I'm sure very painful for him. His is taking this path under duress and I suspect will be rebellious at times. Thanks for your patience.

The only question I have is whether three days are enough. Since he can't be with you every couple of months (and I am distanced from him), should we have him stay an extra day for insurance? He could come up on Wednesday evening and spend Thursday through Saturday and then return to New York late Sunday afternoon, if you could use the extra day.

Of course, I leave it to you, since you have a great deal of experience in handling forced feminization.

Please let's stay in touch and let me know what your thoughts are. I can't wait to enjoy what you will be able to do to help him travel his new path. By the way, since his wife is straight and ignorant of what is going on, we will have to avoid any practices that will make her suspicious. It will be enough that she will be one of the beneficiaries of these improvements. Isn't this fun?

* * *

"Nancy" read a letter to you over the phone and you agreed to my suggestions. Thank you. However, on reading your introductory booklet I suggest you do bare bottom spankings and corner time with bottom on display. This will be excellent for her. The fact that you check them when they have been to the washroom is also very good and should make Nancy squirm.

Any workshops that you think are good for her will be fine with me. The main objective is to give Nancy the most public humiliation possible. You say that only you are authorized to discipline and punish students. In Nancy's case I ask that other mistresses punish her as well, maybe just by spanking with panties on. I leave that to you.

Nancy will, I am sure, enjoy the public humiliation in your warm, safe and non-judgmental atmosphere. She will plead with you not to spank or punish her and not to pull her panties down and make a spectacle herself when being spanked, but she is very submissive and will in reality enjoy every minute of it.

Please ask her about her early experiences with her step sister, step mother and first wife. She is married again, so please leave no marks or redness. Her wife knows nothing of her lifestyle.

Could you please allow her to be dressed and out of the Academy by 3:45? She has a meeting north of the city at 5:00. Thank you. Mistress B.

CHAPTER 13

Take My Man

Just like in the Chapter called "Take My Slave", I say the following. It is likely that some of these were written by the clients themselves as part of their fantasy of having one woman giving him to another for punishment or training. In some cases the letters were from actual mistresses, again catering to the client's fantasy in this regard. Finally, some actually were from wives or girlfriends sending their partner to me. Of these, some may yet again be catering to the man's fantasy, but I know for a fact that a few were genuinely from women who are actually catering to their own desires.

*   *   *

This is my nephew Bobby, who I raised as my own. While he has always been well behaved, I'm afraid his lustful ways have gotten the better of him.

Recently I thought I saw him peeping at me while I was undressing. Another time, while I was doing laundry, I noticed that a pair of my panties had been soiled with what had to have been his semen. When I confronted Bobby, he denied everything.

Then last night I dozed off on the couch while watching television with Bobby. When I awoke, I discovered his hand on my breast while his other hand was stroking his erect penis.

I yelled at him and of course Bobby apologized, promising never to misbehave again. I would like to believe him, but just to be sure I am sending Bobby to you so that you can impart to him the discipline he requires. After all, you are the experts. I trust Bobby will respond well to your instruction and will return often to your splendid Academy.

P.S: Please send me a note home with Bobby letting me know how he did. In order to ensure his full cooperation, I warned him that he will not be allowed back in our home without a satisfactory report.

*   *   *

It was my idea to send my husband back to "school" or to an institution that is able to develop his talents. Even separated, I'm still interested in his well-being and happiness. Yes, I still love him in a special way. There are many reasons why I moved away from him.

I simply do not possess the time to train him for domestic duties or social behavior. It is rather difficult to train him for anything. Certainly, I do like the idea of giving him another chance to spend occasional time with me as my houseboy or butler after a proper training in servitude by someone of female authority. Here are some attitudes that require correction:

First, his efforts to listen patiently to me when I have to explain simple or important issues are not sufficient. His thoughts are elsewhere, mostly with his work and hobbies. The time he spends on our computer seems endless. It got so bad that I had to ask him three times to clean the kitchen and wash the dishes.

Second, he wears old jeans and old track suits around me way too often and is too cheap to buy himself new clothes. He tells me he needs to relax.

Third, he hates going to parties and just wants to spend time by himself. What about me? He actually answered me back when I wanted to invite my friends for a dinner meeting. Can you believe that?

Fourth, his reluctance to go shopping with me really got out of hand. He proposed to drop me off at the mall. Gee!

Fifth, sometimes he ignores me! More than once I got angry at him and ordered him into our bedroom to strip naked. I had no problem tying him up to administer a hefty caning.

The change in his attitude for a few days because of your training was remarkable. But it always just lasts a few days. I tried to deny him my administration of the daily milking (I stopped having intercourse with him years ago), but that did not yield any positive response. He did not even beg me for it. I actually surprised him jerking off at the computer. Only when I resumed masturbating him did he leave his state of remoteness and did I get his attention back.

I'm sure he will follow you or any other mistress of your institution and stay the course like a puppy pet, if he remains maintained. I read about the policy of [*she mentions a dominatrix who wrote an article*] regarding this process and found it very convincing. It is securing our power and dominance over the lowly male.

I do not have the patience for him anymore. His training will consume way too much time and effort, so please help him not to become a social outcast. After all, he is a very kind and gentle soul. Also, make sure that he has to stay at least a couple of times in your slave camp. Make any escape for him impossible. It might be a good idea to store his clothes away for most of his educational stays or, better, some sort of bondage at all times. I'm not sure if my mental ties will be enough for him to stay the course. I simply have to put my trust into you and your capable staff. It would be nice to enjoy a finished product for a change.

*   *   *

I had to virtually rewrite the following letter because it was so poorly written. I told her to send me the money and I would send the e-mail. There was no response.

I was so surprised to see those photos. I really got excited thinking about how my guy would look if he was got up like one of those maids. Well Headmistress, I want him to be a good respectful maid and I think I am going to send him to you and I won't hesitate giving money to you to make him a good submissive maid. I would also love you to be strict with him because I am a feminist. I believe the world turns around us. I can write a strict letter to him about how he should behave, but I want him to learn from you, and I think you should write it. You can write the letter to his e-mail. I would love to see him reading it so this silly little boy will see what is going to happen to him.

*   *   *

After viewing you Web site I am thinking about the training of my slave husband. Your school may be the place he needs to attend. Please advise me as to the cost for thirty or sixty days of your training. I want him to become trained as a sissy maid so he may better please me. I have done a lot of his training, but he needs more. I'm looking for the perfect slave to serve me. He is not perfect. I so much thank you for your time in considering him. As time allows please let me hear from you.

* * *

I e-mailed you in December regarding my husband's trip to Toronto this spring to attend a seminar. I am also interested in having him attend your Sissy Maid Academy for a day or two while he is there. He likes to be my "maid" around the house at times, but I am seriously considering making his duties more regular and mandatory. It would sure help me and I'm all for it. However I think he still needs some basic training in the matter and I would welcome the opportunity for him to attend some of your classes and, upon his return, have him report back to me what he has learned. I'm also interested in him experiencing some corset training so he can appreciate how difficult it may actually be to be a house maid. Please let me know what you can provide for his training and what I need to do to schedule his visit to your Academy. I'm pretty sure I can convince him to attend and follow your training and punishment as you see fit, and I need you to start working on him as soon as possible. Thanks for your assistance.

* * *

Thank you for considering our application to your fine school. My husband is a fifty-five year old cross-dresser and has been wearing women's clothes for as long as I have known him. Over the years he's gotten pretty good at it and is passable from a distance. He goes out once or twice a week but avoids large crowds.

We have been married for thirty-three years and I am 100% supportive of his cross-dressing. I help him shop, alter his clothes, style his hair and make maid outfits for him. He is an excellent provider and a fine man, so I have no problem accommodating him with this behavior in private.

Like most cross-dressers, his fantasy has always been to be forced to wear women's clothes. The maid fantasy is particularly appealing to him. He says he would love to be forced to serve a group of women as their maid. This is not possible for us here at home. They should have total control over him and use light bondage as well as other punishments to control his behavior.

When we are in Canada, as a treat to him, we would like to spend a day at your school with the morning devoted to an introduction to maid service and the afternoon spent in public, perhaps on a tour of Toronto with him cross-dressed. I hope that he will learn to be more submissive and more feminine and that I will become comfortable in a dominant role, not just supportive.

*   *   *

I was very surprised that you responded to my call so quickly. It was a very nice surprise. I am looking for a fun and exciting place to train my slave/sissy husband. We came upon your company by surprise and it looks like it might just be the place for us.

She then asked me about companies that sell merchandise relating to slave training and so forth.

Is your academy is only for cross-dressers, or is it for slave training in general? Also, you mentioned something about a dungeon. Can you send more information about that part of your training? Please send more information about your bed and breakfast and what someone like me can enjoy while I have my slave trained.

CHAPTER 14

Make Me a Dominatrix

Women applied to me for jobs, or to be trained in dominating men non-professionally. Some just came in and talked to me about it. Some filled in an application and gave me a resume. Some also wrote letters or e-mails. I have represented some of these applications below. I relied only on written material, which I present here in letter form.

* * *

Some day this girl hopes to get there to learn to be a good bitch. She needs a weekend assisting Madame de Sade so she can learn to be the best little bitch she can be. Let me know some dates so I can book my plane.

* * *

I am looking for a place or a mistress who can train me in the art of dominating men. I have been a slave over the past year and have recently turned to the domination side, and have enjoyed it. I am more interested in being a dom and learning more techniques to use on my slave/sissy maid. I do not want to become a professional dom. I am looking for new techniques to use in the privacy of my own home. If you can help me with the information I'm looking for it would be greatly appreciated.

* * *

This young lady was financially independent and a college student nearby. She had traveled in the summers, and had previously worked for some time with one of my fellow doms. She had the freedom to live as she wished. She did not have to worry about making a full living. She was an excellent dominatrix for me. She has remained in the profession.

It has been for so very long that I have wished to share my secret passion of becoming a mistress again. The day has arrived that I must rise again, ready to prepare for the coronation of domination and give birth to the priestess within. Perhaps it has to do with the life I lived long ago. When I put on my boots I feel almost immortal, powerful, supernatural, and ready to rule my kingdom and be worshipped. I am ready to train and earn my keep with you.

*   *   *

I found that advertising for doms was good for business in that they often brought a following, which was good business for the house. It was also a way to keep an eye out for talented and reliable gals.

I spoke to you, or a staff member, over the phone recently about the advertisement you had in the paper looking for people to hire. I've enclosed a photo of myself and here is a brief bio. I'm in my early twenties, five foot seven, about 120 pounds. My real eyes are hazel, but I have a different colored set of contact lenses for every day of the week. I usually prefer violet or white-out like in the photo because they're freaky. I usually have some kind of multicolored hair extensions, but my hair is really black and down to my waist when I wear it down.

I would really jump at the chance to get more use of my fetish wear collection. I have a closet full of leather, rubber, and PVC clothing (Hey, it's a fetish) which I usually wear at Goth or fetish clubs and parties. They are appreciated in places like these. I am knowledgeable about the many aspects of the fetish scene, but I have not practiced it professionally, thus I would be very excited to be trained in many different areas. You asked me over the phone what I will do and won't do, so here is my list.

I am definitely a top. I am most comfortable being in control or, for training purposes, I would very much like to assist a person who is in control. I can see from your Web site that you have various different role play scenarios. I'm comfortable with most of what I saw on your Web site, not as a sub though. Playing a nurse, bondage and discipline and dungeon play are all o.k. I might also be convinced to play as an extra for some scenarios (say if you need an extra student in the classroom). I will play with other girls. As for other things, I've got to have left some things out. They would have to be discussed. There are probably many more things I have to learn about that I am unaware of that I would have to discuss. Oh, the woes of being naïve.

Now for the things I will not do. First, I will take no sex or penetration of any kind. I also don't wish to partake in any activities that deal with bodily excrement. If these are things you didn't want to hear, I'm sorry you had to read this far, but I'm being honest.

As I specified before, I will need training. I don't have experience in the professional environment, but I pick things up quickly and would make an intelligent and inquisitive trainee. Oh, and if anything ever gets out of hand for you guys (which I'm sure they don't) I have years of martial arts training and have taken down some very big boys in the ring.

If you need any questions answered please feel free to e-mail me at any time and I will answer them promptly. Thanks for your time and consideration.

* * *

Hi! I've always been an avid supporter of what you are doing. I was impressed when I recently saw you on television. Could you let me know if there are any possibilities for employment with your agency in the near future?

* * *

My experience with BDSM to this point has been somewhat superficial. They have included bondage, blindfolds, and spanking men by hand, paddle and riding crop. I now wish to gain a complete understanding of what it is to be a professional dominatrix of the highest order. I want to know all about the implements and psychology.

Spiritually my beliefs fall between [*she named two religions*]. I have a great love of "Mother Earth" as well as a compassion for all beings. I am willing to switch from dom to sub as the opportunity arises, as long as I am learning to be the best dom I can be. Please know the majority of money I make will go to the attainment of the proper wardrobe and implements.

*   *   *

I am twenty-nine years old and studying design arts and visual media at university, part time. I am also a part time mistress and would love to work for you. I am willing to do scenes, as a top, involving gags, cuffs and harnesses. I like to spank, flog and cane. I have recently completed a caning workshop. I am currently learning the use of the bull whip. I enjoy humiliating and shaming. I can also role play as a mother, aunt, babysitter, governess and school mistress. I am not willing to engage in sexual acts or be naked. I enjoy being a bottom in my personal life, but I am not yet comfortable bottoming within a professional context. These are the major categories I can summon up at the moment. I know there is much, much more, and the extent of possibilities is only limited to the imagination.

*   *   *

I work in the management of fine arts productions and have had extensive private musical and dance training. I have recently attended workshops on flogging. I currently work in a massage parlor where I also do spankings and cater to foot fetishists. I worked as an escort for a year and during that experience did some role playing and catered to the fetishes of some of my clients. I have worked at a well known dungeon for a couple of months but found the conditions unclean and unsafe. I have a personal interest and am an S&M player with my partner at home. I have read several books on the topic as well as erotic literature and have an interest in learning more about S&M, human sexuality and behavior.

*   *   *

I am a fifty year old widow. My husband died in a car accident several years ago. I have not had the urge to find another husband, let alone consider the dating scene all over again. I am financially secure, so I don't have to work or worry about paying my bills or mortgage. I have been entertaining a fantasy of becoming a professional dominatrix for many months, and am now turning to you for help to make it a reality. I have come to the realization that I do need companionship, a man or perhaps several men around the house to do my bidding.

My husband and I knew a woman who was a professional dominatrix. I was fascinated by her lifestyle, her wardrobe and the way she could command her slaves to do whatever she asked without question. She has since moved away to the U.S. but we are still in touch from time to time. She recommended that I contact you by writing a letter of introduction.

Gracious Madame, I would like to learn how to acquire a stable of slaves and learn to train them to my specifications once I've got them under my control. I understand you offer an apprenticeship program at your house to women who show an interest in becoming a professional dominatrix. I understand there is no sex involved so there is no risk of being busted. I really like that. I do not want to be considered a prostitute or go anywhere near a bawdy house for that matter. I have never been in trouble with the law. I have a degree in liberal arts and travel extensively. I do not want to compromise my passport. I've always kept my nose clean. Please Madame, consider my letter of introduction for a position in your house. I would be eternally grateful to you. This young widow needs a new lease on life. I thank you from the bottom of my heart.

*   *   *

In training the women to be a dominatrix I asked them to look at a list of paraphilia, meaning things that might arouse men. There are over seven hundred and I am going to list thirty for you now. This is just a sample, repeat sample, from the letter A.

Allotriorasty (arousal from partners of other nations or races), Altocalciphilia (high heel fetish), Alvinolagnia (stomach fetish), Amaurophilia (preference for a blind or blindfolded sex partner), Amoaxia (sex in a parked car), Amelotasis (attraction to the absence of a limb), Amokoscisia (desire to slash or mutilate women), Amychesis (act of scratching partner during sex), Amacliism (arousal from items used as an infant), Analingus (rimming or penetration of the anus with the tongue), Amasteemaphilia (attraction to taller or shorter partners), Androidism (arousal from robots with human features), Androminetophilia (arousal from female partners who dress like males), Anililagnia (arousal from older female sex partners), Antholagnia (arousal from smelling flowers), Apotemnophilia (fantasies about losing a limb), Arachnephilia (arousal from spiders), Asphyxiaphilia (arousal from the lack of oxygen), Asthenolagnia (arousal from weakness or being humiliated), Autagnoistophilia (exhibitionism, arousal from exposing one's naked body or genitals to strangers while on a stage or while being photographed), Autassassinophilia (arousal from orchestrating one's own death at the hands of another), Autogynephilia (arousal from cross-dressing), Automasochism (arousal from inflicting intense sensations or pain on one's own body), Automysophilia (arousal from being dirty or defiled), Autonepiophilia (infantilism, arousal from dressing or being treated like an infant), Autopederasty (person inserting their own penis into their anus), Autophagy (self cannibalism, or eating one's own flesh), Auto Sadism (infliction of pain or injury on oneself), Avisodomy (breaking the neck of a bird while penetrating it for sex), Axillism (penis penetrating an armpit).

*   *   *

I held a weekly seminar for prospective and existing employees at my house in Toronto on Saturday or Sunday afternoons for about eighteen months. I prepared notes and published materials which I gave to them, in addition to lecturing, answering questions and giving demonstrations. Here is a brief excerpt from those notes, written by me, where I tried to convey the impression a dominatrix would make on a client.

The dominatrix obeys nothing but the conviction of her own grandeur. The dominatrix styles herself a Lucifer. The dominatrix speaks with the conviction that whatever she says is correct. The dominatrix has a shell of authority and recognizes attack as the key. The dominatrix taps into her death dealing instincts. The dominatrix conveys the impression of control. The dominatrix does nothing to dissuade her slaves from their submission, for when she torments them she no longer feels self hatred. The dominatrix knows a morbid satisfaction in clinging to the idea that she posses a special sensibility that penetrates and loves the secretive. The dominatrix is created in the image of cruelty, so that her victims realize their victim's nature in groveling before the Goddess. The dominatrix conveys an enjoyment of her lifestyle. The dominatrix possesses a great deal of wicked wit. The dominatrix has a flair for sensations. The dominatrix has manners of expression that are overpowering. The dominatrix does not show remorse. The dominatrix has great sexual appeal whether fit or fat. The dominatrix strives to strengthen her individuality. The dominatrix exalts her passions. The dominatrix is adventurous. The dominatrix is uniformed. The dominatrix conveys that she is an unattainable object of desire and worship.

*   *   *

I prepared a manual for those enrolled in the Millicent Farnsworth Sissy Maid Academy. Here are some excerpts from the manual entitled "The Millicent Farnsworth Sissy Maid Academy and Charm School for Gentlemen in Need of Behavior Modification through Forced Feminization and Domestic Discipline".

It has become increasingly apparent that our social traditions are rapidly changing. The time has arrived for the effeminate submissive male to take his proud place in society as The Sissy Maid. The ongoing paradigm shift in women's attitudes and career concepts has created a new social and professional niche for the Sissy Maid and the women they love to serve. These changes have led me to introduce The Millicent Farnsworth Sissy Maid Academy.

The following are the Academy's Rules and Regulations. You will always address me as Headmistress or Madame. You must accurately report all administrative information concerning your physical health, mental health, emotional state, limits and expectations prior to your acceptance. Students will wait in their designated sissy corner until summoned to assembly, class, duties or the Headmistress's office. Students are required to read materials in the Sissy Maid Training Room containing all rules and regulations of the Academy before assembly. All students must be males cross-dressed as females. All students must show a willingness to learn and please the Headmistress. All students must display a pleasant disposition. Unnecessary and inappropriate touching or physical contact will cause a student to be expelled or sent to the punishment room. Eyes must remain downcast when in the presence of the Headmistress.

Those were some of the forty rules. Needless to say infractions were so numerous that punishment was frequently required. A list of twenty-two infractions was also provided, but space does not permit me to list them. Here are some more excerpts from the manual:

The following workshops are for students at the Academy: transformations, communicating, voice lessons, manners, coquette, social behavior, developing a feminine personality, history lessons, acting like a girl, role playing and the private theater, what to read, becoming a female impersonator, personal secretary training, poise and confidence, walking, sitting, standing, keeping a daily diary, hair and wig care, makeup lessons, hand and foot care, skin care and nail care.

This form states that you have consented to allow The Headmistress to oversee your full instruction. Should you disobey The Headmistress or any of her delegates, you will learn to understand the meaning of discipline, verbal reprimand, corporal punishment and humiliation. Maid training is serious business. Insolence will not be tolerated. You will agree to comply with humble obedience to all rules and regulations of the Academy. We expect people of the highest caliber to enroll in our Academy. You may now sign.

What followed after that were many pages listing the duties of various roles they might assume, an application form, a questionnaire and various relevant articles taken from publications.

CHAPTER 15

Thank You Mistress

Letters written after the clients visited were generally very gratifying to get. I never got a negative one. That is the truth. No client ever even told me they thought they had been ripped off. The gals who worked for me also, to this day, have positive things to say. I am especially pleased to share these letters with you.

* * *

Well, my Toronto adventure is over, I am home again standing up to pee. This is a short note to once more say how much I enjoyed my visit and to thank you for your kindness and attention.

From you and the others, I sensed a sincere and genuine interest in me, meaning my enjoyment and that you both truly enjoyed the interaction with me as an individual. I quickly came to like you all very much. This is not necessary to having a successful encounter/session, but your personalities and caring, that prompt the affection, are wonderful bonuses, tremendously raising the satisfaction level and my desire to return. It made my decision to extend my visit come early and easily.

I'm sitting here thinking through the week's activities—and it is the neat and interesting people I met that come most to mind. The things I did, especially the Tuesday night trip, were exciting, but it is you and the others that I'll remember most. You were genuine and adapted to keep the fantasy working. I never felt I was simply moving through a script: you continually showed an interest in how I was responding. You seemed to naturally find the balance between dominance and accommodation. I think that reflects both your experience and values as a person. I received much more than I expected and am grateful. Ah, and I must mention my surprise at how good the food was and at Suzy's skill as a cook, although I admit to some lingering effects from her wonderful beans.

I hope to write a sort of narrative story of my adventure, but am off on another trip in a couple of days and won't have it immediately. So I will end the quick note of thanks now rather than wait until I have time for a story. Again, thanks; good luck and I am looking forward to a return visit.

* * *

This note was sent by a female client. I still remember how amazingly turned on she was being dominated by other women. She told me she was a successful, young, single, professional straight woman who was too shy and frightened to act out her fantasies with dates.

Here it is, two weeks since visiting and still the time spent at the academy continues to occupy much of my thinking or daydreaming, especially about the time spent chained to the bed. I feel bad about "whimping out" on the nipple clamps, since I have used others for about an hour (while standing up). Next time I must try them standing up and really wear them for the hour!

I promised to send you a few Web site addresses that may be of interest. First two Web sites, one that deals with corsets and the other with petticoats [*the sites are given*]. Both sites are run by the same group, offer numerous historical/how to use articles and have links to suppliers and pictures. These next two sites deal with chastity belts from a historical perspective, current use and fiction. The second site went down recently but as of today seems to be back up. These two chastity belt sites have links to many other sources and manufacturers [*the sites are given*]. I hope you find these sites useful. Thanks again.

* * *

This letter, written in 1998, when I had just begun to reopen, came via regular mail. You will note how he says I have his phone and fax number. He was becoming the exception in this respect. It was amazing how the Internet was becoming more and more common in the late 1990's. When I was put out of business in late 1994 I did not know anyone who had Internet access from home. By 1998 I would say that almost half of the people I spoke to about it had access from their home, and many others had it at their office. One of the first things I did when setting up in 1998 was to set up the Web site.

Thank you so much for making my brief stay a truly memorable experience. I am so sorry that I had to leave early. By the time I arrived back in Chicago on Friday night my cold was really upon me. I spent Sunday and yesterday home in bed. I'm back at work this morning and feeling much better.

While I did not meet all your staff, I cannot imagine any way that my visit could have been better. You truly gave me a deep comfort level. I really am looking forward to my next visit with you, particularly the maid training you mentioned.

Being at home for the past couple of days really allows one some good thinking time. For me, I kept coming back to my Friday with you. Thinking how nervous I was upon arrival and almost immediately being put at ease by your manner. Then when you selected the red wig for me without me ever telling you it is my favorite color was uncanny. This was followed by your suggestion for a maid's outfit. This gave me the opportunity to tell you of my fantasy to be a maid. It was almost as if you were in my head deciding what I should say next. A truly great day!

Now for the red dress. I simply have to have it. Unfortunately you did not have any available for sale. Is there any way that the dress I wore can be sold to me? I do not care that others have worn it. When I was in that dress, it was me. Talk to me about this please. You should have my phone and fax numbers in your records.

I am looking forward to hearing from you regarding the maid training. As soon as you fill me in I will schedule this with you, the sooner the better. I am excited.

Again, thank you for a wonderful day. I will cherish every moment. I look forward to hearing from you and arranging my next visit. Happy holidays to you and yours.

*   *   *

I just wanted to let you know how pleased I was with my husband over the holidays. "Bonnie Sue" was a big help in doing all the housework for me while I was at work. "She" even baked and iced most of the cookies. I can't believe how much of an improvement there has been in "her" attitude.

Thanks for the pictures. They were very entertaining. I printed off copies and I have them in a safe place in case I need them at a later date if there is a slackening off in "her" performance.

With the kids at home over the holidays, it is impossible to have "her" dressed in the proper attire, but even so it's sure nice to have a dedicated man maid to do most of the household chores. I don't know how long it will be before the chores actually become chores, but after the holidays I am going to look into getting an outfit for him so that I can take some more pictures for insurance for when "she" starts to complain or realizes that "her" place is now serving instead of being served.

* * *

Thank you for the wonderful job you are doing with Bobby. He obviously enjoys being spanked and disciplined by beautiful women, especially when his penis is put on display in the process. Being teased and used as a plaything while receiving punishment shows Bobby that women are allowed to amuse themselves at his expense. The more you point out how aroused this makes him, the more effective the training.

For today's lesson, Bobby has brought a package. He doesn't know that inside is something for him to wear. This is a new form of humiliation for Bobby and he may require your help to get him over his reluctance. Slap his face if you must, but be sure he wears the outfit. Have him model it for you and instruct him on how to parade around in it like the slut that he is.

In fact, let's call him Barbie, shall we? If he needs to be convinced, just show him how aroused he gets when his nipples are pinched. Perhaps you could have him demonstrate for you how he would give oral pleasure to a man. Now that would be embarrassing, wouldn't it?

If all goes well, take him into your bedroom. Sit on the edge of the bed and lay him across your lap. A long, loving spanking will be his reward.

* * *

I just wanted to offer you a short letter in order to thank you for granting me permission to grovel at your feet and for allowing me the time to succumb to your every wish and command. As you could probably see, I require much more training in order to properly gratify my Mistress. I hope that I did not displease you in any way, and that I performed as you expect all your little boys and girls to.

I would like to express my gratitude for introducing me to the lovely world of discipline, bondage, servitude and all other delightful forms of fetishes and sweet perversions. I don't know how to adequately display my appreciation, but I'm quite sure that you will be able to think of some chores and duties that will allow me to show my thankfulness. Perhaps you would enjoy something that involved some of your other slaves, male and/or female.

I hope this letter and the photos don't cross any of your boundaries, but if so, I'm sure that the next time you allow me into your home, you will remind me of what proper etiquette is and what is not.

* * *

I just wanted to wish you luck with your court case. I think that you should, and will eventually win. The services you provide are needed in this community. One day I hope to have the nerve to visit you for maid training and discipline.

* * *

I called in to you when you were on television last night. I told you on air that I supported you all the way. When they accuse you of sex acts or whatever it is so wrong. If a woman wears a blouse with a couple of buttons undone and a man gets turned on, should she also be accused of sex acts? The same goes when women cross their legs. This turns some men on.

They seem to be persecuting you for providing a service other than sex to men who have natural instincts. They are in effect saying all people are guilty. We are all human and entitled to have emotions and feelings. Nobody has the right to tell us what to feel or how to manage our fantasies.

I work with a submissive man (*the writer is a woman*) who I am in the process of feminizing, and I love what I do. Too bad more female dominants didn't call in to support you. Keep up what you are doing. It doesn't hurt anyone. I would love it if you sent me an e-mail with your thoughts on things.

Doesn't hurt anyone? She has obviously never been on the end of my whip.

* * *

This letter is of particular interest to me now. It was written in 1993, when I ran the Bondage Bungalow, subject of the famous raid in late 1994 and trials in the ensuing years. It gives us comments from a client after his first visit. Such correspondence is very rare because this was before the Internet came into use He refers to Marie. I was known for most scenarios as Mistress Marie, even though the place was called Madame de Sade's. He was writing to Madame de Sade, who, unknown to him, was me. His letter was lengthy and hand written. He wrote very well, and obviously took time over it. I have excerpted about half of the letter.

These are my random thoughts relating to my initial visit to the fantasy chamber of Mistress Marie and [*he named one of the other doms*] yesterday. They were exciting contrasts in sexuality. One was voluptuous and quietly dominant (*That was me. Before I got sick I was much heavier*). The other was petite and enthusiastically demanding. There was the one with a charming smile and twinkling, guaranteed to seduce any man into submission, and the other with a tantalizing body suggesting erotic misadventures. The latter was very distracting and ensured total obedience from me, the lusting submissive.

I was very impressed by the skilled interactive role playing between the two mistresses. Such squeals of delight when their comments or actions surprised or frightened me! I loved their apparent enjoyment in trying to outdo each other in teasing, humiliating and disciplining the confessed submissive. I loved the fun they seemed to be having in providing the fantasy. It was as if all the props and their submissive were there only for their amusement and enjoyment.

They were very adept at making the fantasy realistic, and hence more enjoyable. The rooms were incredible: the jail cell, classroom, altar and examination room in particular. I wonder why they have a television and video cassette recorder in the classroom. Could it be for visual aid instruction for slave training, body worship or oral devotion courses?

I can't believe that I endured (enjoyed?) the prolonged vigorous whipping by Marie. God is she ever proficient with those instruments! Her skill and ability in knowing how to stretch a man's limits for pain are clearly evident. I was so impressed by her soft spoken requests for me to count the lashes for her and that no amount of pleading on my part was going to alter the punishment—the whipping was inevitable. She took me to further limits by whispering encouragement of how well I was reacting to my slave training experience. I kind of wish that the other one had been standing before me to see that I wasn't a wimp who was unable to absorb the punishment. But come to think of it, lusting for her beautiful body and seeing her insipid smile as she paraded before me might have taken my mind off the stinging discipline a little.

It was an exciting experience! I wonder if I can wait four to six weeks before I long for my next dominant fantasy.

* * *

Last night's session for two hours with Mistress Cintra was a great event! You were right when you smiled when I asked if she could go heavy. I don't have Cintra's e-mail address to thank her directly. Could you do so for me please?

I would love to watch a session with Cintra and [*he named another dom*] for an hour. This would involve clamps and waxing with some discipline. Could you give me an idea of the fee? I do not really want to participate in this; simply viewing at close hand is fine. Cintra was unsure of exactly what the other girl's limits are.

Unfortunately, because of the season, I will not be available for a session until sometime in January. Until then, best regards.

* * *

This letter was hand written.

Thank you for sending me a report card on my progress thus far. It really shows me the aspects of my classes I need to concentrate on. I promise to practice to become the best sissy-maid I can, and hopefully make you proud of me. I am hoping that the essay I have sent will qualify as my homework assignment and hopefully will show that I am trying to anticipate your wishes. If you find this is not acceptable please write me back and I will gladly do another essay. I am extremely excited about my visit to the Sissy Maid Academy and can't wait to return, hopefully in September. I will now start my punishment phase and hope this meets with your satisfaction.

I will learn perfect obedience. I am a bad little sissy maid.

He wrote that out 100 times.

Headmistress, after writing this out so many times I must tell you that I completely put my fate in your hands. I trust you Headmistress with any assignment you may give me. Please allow me to serve you in any way you see fit.

* * *

Discipline and well entrenched male thought patterns were the two elements I discovered today. The degree of punishment to grab attention and to correct behavior was strong and unrelenting. It certainly reveals the weaknesses of my male tendencies in a dramatic manner. Just as I thought I was making headway a breakdown occurred and you pounced on it, which was a most effective means to attack poor behavior. The dungeon was interesting and beneficial for greater humiliation, but I prefer pure bondage for sensual purposes which better connect me to my feminine personality.

* * *

Last June you helped me get made up and dressed up as a lady. It was an enjoyable experience, but mostly it just felt right. It was exciting and erotic, but the overwhelming feeling was wholeness and the feeling that "This is something that should be." I have enclosed a snapshot of that day and you can include it in your album if you wish. It's not the best photo of the day. I've kept those good ones, and the fellow taking the photos rarely got close enough to get good photos anyway.

The reason I am writing is that I just read a profile about you in the October 1999 edition of Chatelaine Magazine [*he saw it many months after it was published*] and I want to offer my support for your battle in the courts. I'm not in any kind of position to help financially, not even close, but I wanted to let you know that I think that the battle you're fighting is important and right.

For me the time at your place was a one-time extravagance to celebrate starting a new job after being out of work for many months and suffering stress related illnesses. I have started a new job, paying less but less stressful. It is in a small town and I walk to work.

I think in some part my stress came from being always forced to deny who and what I am or want to be. Since last summer, when I saw myself dressed and made up as a beautiful woman, I have been able to feel so much more positive about myself. I feel good when I derive pleasure and a soulful satisfaction wearing my panties, bras, dresses and high heels, and loving the female (and male) part of me. I've stopped the constant beating up of myself and some day look forward to sharing this with more people.

Thank you for being a part of that last June and thank you for what you are doing in the bigger picture of helping people enjoy the freedom and dignity of being who they are.

Pleasure to meet you

Pleasure to beat you

PART 2

Being a Dominatrix

CHAPTER 16

A Day in My Life: Wednesday June 9, 1993

I want to tell you about how I brought to life some of the fantasies in the letters you've been reading. In my first book I told you about the scenes and what it took to run a role play facility. Now I can take you through a single day, all twenty-four hours, leaving out nothing. First I'll give you some history and context.

A Bit of History

I should mention that in my home town of Windsor (a small Canadian city beside Detroit—about four hours from Toronto) I ran an escort service from a warehouse studio I rented. There was a small cellar that I converted into a dungeon. I was the only one who did fetish clients. I was busted in 1986 after a couple of years in business. I moved to Toronto in 1990 after doing jail time near Toronto and supported myself working in massage parlors, office jobs or collecting unemployment insurance. I visited some of the few houses of domination in Toronto, sometimes to apply for a job and sometimes posing as a client to see their premises. I also considered setting up on my own when I could save up a bit of money. I remembered how safe it was to work from home. I was also very aware that I was into my thirties, so work as an escort and so forth was not going to pay.

The economics were actually quite simple. Let's say I had a house or even an apartment that I rented. If I saw one client a day I could pay the rent, advertising, and build up some equipment and clothing. If I saw two I could even put aside some money. I also knew that with a business partner I could split the overhead and we could make sure no appointments were lost, and my partner and I could even earn extra income from a job outside the business we were running. Above all, I concluded that I must be in charge. The girls who worked for other doms told me it did not pay well to work for other doms. I also knew from experience that a larger premises with more elaborate props would pay better than, say, a small apartment.

So I bided my time and looked at properties and lived on as little as I could. I got a job in telemarketing and became friends with a gal who seemed a first rate person. She was blond, slim and beautiful. She was also down on her luck due, of course, to a guy leaving her. She had a male friend who was not her boyfriend. His name was Edward, or Ed. Ed was a handyman with lots of experience, who had just landed a major job. A property speculator, a very rich older man, who I will call Jerry, had just bought what I later found out was a house on the largest residential lot in Thornhill, just north of Toronto. Real estate prices were depressed and he got it very cheaply. I remember reading after I was raided that the property was worth $1.5 million at its lowest point in the market cycle. Like I said, cheaply. Wow!

Jerry hired Ed for a job he said would probably take at least two years, but may last much longer than that. He also said he would give Ed a big lump sum when the job was over. The terms were that Ed could live on the property for free while he worked to rehabilitate the grounds and renovate the house and garage. That meant that Jerry paid the property taxes, utilities and gave Edward a fund for materials and supplies. All Ed needed to do was earn money outside to pay for his food and any other incidentals.

The Rise of the Bondage Bungalow

I met Ed and told him I wanted to run a role play facility. I told him it would not be too much of an intrusion if I ran it in the house he was to renovate, and that when I was not busy with clients I would help him with his work. I told him I would pay him a set amount as rent and he could share in the income from the business. He agreed and said he was also willing to work as security. He had the size and the look. So, we had a deal. My lady friend also agreed to spend some time there as an assistant and dominatrix in training. It meant some extra income for her.

Ed told Jerry that I would be running a modest beauty treatment business and helping him with the work on the house and grounds. I met Jerry who said he was very sympathetic to working people making a living, and said he was glad for me. I think that he was also glad that Ed, who was a bit shy, would be living with a woman. Ed assured me that Jerry would not visit often, and we could set things up so that it could be made to look very innocent within a short time, if anyone came to inspect the place. We could even tell Jerry, if he became suspicious, that we were just playing among ourselves and friends. Finally, Ed said that Jerry spent many months down south in the winter. He owned a number of properties and rarely visited them. He had relied on Ed before and trusted Ed to report anything that needed reporting. So it looked like a great set-up for my business.

But that place sure needed attention. We moved in very late in 1992. I kept my telemarketing job, which was only about twenty hours a week done in two shifts, so I had cash. For the first month Ed and I collected and cut branches of trees that had fallen or that needed cutting. That was the first order of business, to be done before spring. The days were short so we gathered and cut and took the wood to a big steel dumpster at the front of the house during daylight, but also storing up a vast amount which we could use for fires out back during the summer. Ed would cut and I would gather and we would both carry the wood to the dumpster in the driveway, which was up to about two hundred yards from the back end of the property. The key was to finish before the spring thaw. We finished by mid-March.

In the evenings or when it was too cold or snowing too hard to work outside we worked on the inside of the house. We were both happy. Ed too had had a hard life and the peace and control we had were precious to us both. In time, when Ed saw me with the clients and so forth, he realized we were not boyfriend and girlfriend material, but he was loyal to me and we have remained friends ever since those early days. He was, as I say, very shy and quiet.

After Ed had done the necessary plumbing we had a nice washroom and shower. Then he fixed up a couple of rooms in the basement which served as a dungeon. I gave Ed some specifications and he built a couple of spanking benches and bondage tables, each with o-rings. I also bought some whips and chains, metal clasps, a couple of pairs of high black boots and some dungeon implements. An early client was a carpenter. He built me a couple of jail cells, with wooden bars, in return for his sessions. He even provided the lumber and built a very elaborate suspension system in one of the rooms. I also went on a shopping spree for women's clothes that would fit men. So, as you can see, the place was continuously developing.

I placed some ads and the business came quickly. I gave good value to clients for their money in terms of the time and attention I could give them, compared to when I became busier. When the clients came those parts of the house not worked on yet were draped off, but every day the place was made more presentable. It was good. I felt secure and not fearful of the future. I enjoyed being a dominatrix. I loved the facility that was being created. I loved the quiet neighborhood and the view out the back into the woods from the window in what eventually became my office. I loved working on the grounds, clearing the wood in the winter and planting the garden in the spring. I was pleasantly busy, not bored and not under pressure. It was one of the best times in my otherwise hard life.

I won't go into any more detail, but will just say that by the spring of 1993 my Bondage Bungalow was essentially up and running and business was expanding. Ed was making progress on the property, turning his attention to the outside of the house and the grounds for the next 6 months. Jerry visited briefly a couple of times. He said it might be five years before the property recovered its value, so he and Ed and I agreed that we would give him a good rent after a couple of years if we stayed longer. Jerry said not to worry, after all costs and so forth was considered he expected to make a profit of at least $2 million when he sold the property. Wow! He was very pleased that the eyesore that the property had been became more presentable, and he said he trusted us.

Well, I said I was running a beauty business, and I guess we could have been more honest with Jerry. But Ed and I agreed that we should make sure we made and saved enough money in case the business had to be closed suddenly. Even if Jerry did not give Ed the promised severance, this would mean we would have plenty of time and money to make the next transition in our lives. We even developed an elaborate story to tell Jerry, if he saw everything. We would tell him that friends of ours had us set up the place for them to shoot videos, so we could make some extra money. We actually had a video camera there, as one friend, the carpenter in fact, liked Ed to film his sessions with me.

For me, the top priority was to send money to Windsor for the care of my daughter in her foster home. This I was now able to do. Her foster parents were now able to do even better by her. She also got nice gifts from me when I visited her, which I could now also afford to do more often. I would go down for a couple of days at a time and my daughter and I spent time together at a nice hotel. I told her that one day we would be together again, but I told her I didn't have a place of my own yet and she had to stay in school for a few more years. She had her own life there and seemed to understand.

So that's where things stood as May turned to June in 1993.

Wednesday June 9, 1993

I rarely use my alarm clock. I have to be prepared for calls late at night. Sometimes clients want to stay all night and will pay well for it and can not be left alone all night. I also have to be prepared for calls early in the morning, so clients can schedule their day. In time of course I would have a secretary and receptionist, who I could forward the phone to and so forth. But business had not yet reached that point. Besides, I know that it's rare for calls to come after eleven at night and before seven in the morning, so I'm usually able to sleep then, but of course with the phone in the charger beside me. I sometimes do use my alarm clock though. If I have a client in the morning, or I'm taking a nap, I make sure I set it so I don't oversleep.

However today I have no morning client and the phone does not start ringing early. I have no appointment booked until one o'clock and then two tours of my facility booked later. The tours are $25 and last only fifteen minutes, but often the client will stay for a consultation or even a session as well, and it will turn out to be a profitable appointment. Of course the day is yet young and I might have a full evening of sessions. I get out of bed at nine. I make the bed very carefully and have a shower and dress in my outdoor work clothes. Ed is not a big sleeper. He sleeps downstairs and I sleep upstairs. He has had his coffee and is out back pruning a tree. He is in the middle of a big paint job on part of the outside of the house, but he will not apply paint until all moisture has dried from the night's condensation. I offered to paint for an hour or so in the morning. That will be mid-morning.

It's a sunny and dry morning, perfect temperature. I go to the patio in the back and have my coffee, which Ed made, and a cigarette. I just sit there, taking in the quiet and beauty of it all. No pressure, no fear. Things are going well. (I still remember that morning clearly. It's a sustaining memory for me to this day. I did not know that morning that I was infected with a chronic liver disease, or would be having two partial hysterectomies a few years later. My daughter's situation in her foster home was still, as far as I knew, going well. I was not engaged in any legal battles. I felt good and felt good about the future that morning).

I do not go into the little forest where Ed is working. I take the portable phone with me and get out the paints to continue a paint job now that the condensation is dry. I like painting. I had not painted before and it gives me a sense of accomplishment. Ed taught me how to do it well. I get a couple of calls asking about rates and services and so forth and I make a couple of appointments for the evening.

So now I know my schedule for the day, aside from what I might have to do over the phone. I will see a client at 1:00 for two hours, another at 3:00 for one hour and another at 8:00 for one hour. I also have a tour booked for 4:30 and another at 7:00. If the 7:00 guy wants to stay, I might be able to arrange to have two clients at once without one seeing the other. I can also put the phone on voice mail when I am busy with clients. As you can see, it *was* getting busy. It occurs to me again that I might have to hire more help. I already hired, as I mentioned, the lady from the telemarketing job who introduced me to Ed, but that was only for a couple of afternoons a week. At least I didn't have e-mails to worry about. There was not even a computer on the premises and the Internet was not yet available to households.

Just after noon Ed takes over painting for me so I can change for my first client of the day. Ed provides security by being in a room near where I am with the client, but unknown to the client. This is what he often termed his breaks! He is an amazingly industrious worker. I go into the boudoir and off the boudoir is a wardrobe room. It's there I keep my personal clothes, costumes for role play and some of the cross-dressers' clothing.

The client had requested that he pretend to be a poorly behaved student and I am to play the Headmistress of the school. This meant the look of the teacher from the 1950's or 1960's. I put on a long red-haired wig, white blouse, leather gloves and a black leather skirt over a girdle and stockings held up by garters. To finish it off I put on large glasses.

He arrives in a luxury foreign car. I watch him get out and walk up the driveway. He's a little above middle height, well built, grey haired and wearing what was obviously an expensive business suit. He must be been well off, since he had booked a two hour session. Here is what he has asked for.

His scenario is to begin downstairs where he would shower and change into "school clothes", spend time upstairs in the classroom, be taken to the Headmistress's Office (also upstairs) for misbehaving or failing his lessons, and finally end up back downstairs in the torture room or throne room where he would finish his session (or it would finish him). I play two roles and my assistant, the gal I knew from the telemarketing job, will play one. I will be the Headmistress and prior to that I will be a nurse by putting a medical coat over the clothes I had on that I described above. My assistant, "Teacher" would not have to wear anything in particular, but I preferred her to have a conservative look for this scene, by wearing a tight skirt, high heel dress shoes and nylons with seams. The way I was dressed meant I could play Teacher myself if my assistant was not available.

The nurse will inspect the student after the shower while he was naked, she holding a clipboard, shouting (or screaming) instructions at him to bend over and cough, hold up his arms, present his balls for inspection, stand on one foot and so forth. She will note any details on his limitations and preferences not covered in his intake interview and confirm those that were. She will then order him into frilly panties and lead him upstairs to the classroom where Teacher would take over.

Teacher will then order him to stand facing the corner while she writes the ten rules of the school on the blackboard. He is told to read them out loud and then must turn to the wall and recite them from memory. If Teacher had to take a call or leave the room the student would be told to stand in his frilly panties facing the wall until told to do otherwise. When he has memorized the ten rules he is issued his uniform: white pantyhose, white skirt, girdle, bra with pads, blouse, makeup, perfume and a wig. He is taken to the boudoir or parlor and dressed up by Teacher.

Then it's back to class for lessons in how to walk, talk and act like a lady. The student would have a book; a big Webster's Dictionary on his head and was made to walk without it falling off. If it did fall off he got twenty-five whacks on the ass. Eventually he would, if he was a novice, end up in the Headmistress's Office for punishment. He might or might not be put in bondage first. Punishment would usually be spanking by hand, or with an implement or even a whip or cane. If he was not a novice, and requested it, he could be taken to the dungeon and put into heavy bondage and tortured as punishment for being a bad student.

This particular client liked the full treatment and enjoyed having Teacher watch and giggle while the Headmistress administered punishment, as he struggled in the stocks while his feet were held down on the floor and legs held apart by the spreader bar.

He had his session. It went just like it was planned. Then we will let him shower before leaving at the scheduled 3:00.

Just as we leave him to have his shower the door bell rings and the next client is here, ten minutes early. We sit him in the parlor just off the hallway by the front door behind drapes. I usually like to have a client sit alone for a few minutes whenever possible, just to build suspense. When the two hour client is ready to leave he is escorted through the front door. We did not tell him another client is sitting behind the drapes in the other room, so if he speaks there's the chance his voice might be recognized. Also there's the chance that he would look at the license plate of the other car in the driveway (unless the other client came by cab, which about one third of them did). That is why I try to book clients with a one hour gap in between. However in this case it was not possible unless I was willing to lose doing business when I had an assistant with me.

While we show him out Ed comes out from his hiding place and quickly and quietly removes the used towels, wipes over the shower room and equipment with disinfectant and puts everything into place.

The 3:00 client is a pure S&M lover, meaning he liked to be put in bondage and tortured by a cruel and beautiful woman. He wanted me in a full leather outfit, meaning basically a leather cat suit. These are very expensive and I did not have one, but I did have a shiny backless PVC dress, and with thigh high black leather high heel boots on he liked the look very much, and asks me to stay with it for future sessions.

His script called for him to shower and dry himself while I would scream orders and insults at him. I then tell him to get on his knees or belly and crawl to the Throne Room (which was also one of the torture chambers). I handcuff his hands behind his back and sit on the throne while he worships me and kisses my boots as I sit and laugh and tell him how I am going to torture him for not being creative or articulate enough.

After about ten minutes of this I put him over a spanking bench or spanking horse (depending on my mood) and restrain each limb to one corner of the device. My assistant is still here. When I finish restraining him she comes in, giggles and mocks the client for being in trouble and so helpless. She begs me to spare him and not be too severe. I tell her to be silent and only speak to count the lashes or strokes he would receive.

Then I whip, strap and cane him for about fifteen minutes. When I am finished I tell them him I am going out of the room for a few minutes. My assistant, who you may remember was wearing her high heels and stockings and skirt, was parading herself in front of him while I was administering punishment and screaming with joy each time I hit him (again, part of his script). After I leave she mocks him again, tells him that I can not hear them, and then she whips him for a few minutes, laughing all the time. When I return she immediately tells me he tried to escape, but she prevented it. I told her she was a good girl and began his punishment again, again with her parading in front of him, laughing.

Then, wouldn't you know it, the guy coming for the 4:30 tour rings the front door bell at 3:45. I tell my assistant to answer it and put him in the parlor so, like the previous guy he won't see the current client leaving. Then it occurs to me that if I don't make it to the toilet in the next few minutes I'll burst. Of course we don't want either client's illusions destroyed, so it is a time for thinking. My current client still has time in his session, and I like to let them get ready to leave after their time, and not as part of their time. They really notice this and appreciate it. It's good for getting repeat business.

So, here's what I do. I tell him I'm keeping him an extra half hour, no charge, because I'm enjoying myself so much, if he agrees. He of course does. Then I tell him we're giving a tour and the tour client arrived early. He agrees to have a hood put on him so he won't be recognized when the tour client comes through that part of the house and sees him. (I think he appreciates being part of my advertising, in a manner of speaking). I tell my assistant, who had come downstairs after putting the tour client in the parlor, to do an intake interview before the tour and begin the tour in about fifteen minutes, and that I will now accompany her upstairs so I can go to the bathroom. I then put the hood on the client on the spanking horse, instruct him to be quiet and put a couple of clamps on his nipples so he would suffer while I was away. We then go upstairs, my assistant to do the interview, I to you know where. Relief!

Then I head back downstairs, remove his nipple clamps and resume his punishment, screaming and laughing at him as I do so. This is the signal for my assistant to bring the tour client downstairs to begin the tour. Normally we begin a tour upstairs, but this time we wanted to allow the client being punished to begin to get ready to leave not too far beyond his scheduled leaving time. My assistant preceded the tour client into the dungeon and told him that "our slave" couldn't see him, but that he should not speak, lest the slave recognize his voice. When I see the tour client I say "I want him restrained!" My assistant said "But Headmistress, he is only on a tour." I laugh fiendishly then turn away from them and started screaming at my victim again as I whack him, yelling at him to stop squirming or we would do this all night, and so on.

I continue to punish him and scream at him until my assistant comes down to tell me that the tour client has gone. She says he was amazed and couldn't believe the place we had. He wanted to pay to stay, but she told him there were no openings that day. She gave him an appointment for another day.

I then tell my victim that I'm bored with him and order my assistant to release him. He still has his hood on but can hear my heels clicking loud on the stairs as I go up. Of course my assistant tickles him and pinches his nipples and expresses her disappointment at having to let him out of his restraints before she finally undoes them. She leads him to the shower room where his clothes are and tells him to get ready to go and then come upstairs. He does so and she shows him out. He does not see me again, until his next visit. I am in the back yard, in a blocked off area so no neighbor could see me. Few could even if they tried, even if I was out in the open; so vast were these properties—or should I call them estates?

I am returning calls. It takes thirty minutes. Most are the usual questions. I book a one hour session for the weekend. Then I head inside and change into my tour attire (basically a black academic robe), have some supper, and take a nap. My assistant leaves and either the phone or doorbell will wake me up. It is now 5:00 and other than phone calls it should be quiet. Fortunately Ed is there and cleans up quickly. He has the shower room looking unused and wiped off and disinfects the spanking bench and spanking horse. He lightly sprays and vacuums the room and removes the "school clothes" of the client to a gathering area in the furnace room. We do not have a washer or dryer. We collected what needed washing or dry cleaning and Ed and I would go to a nearby laundry facility once a week or so. Some of the stuff could be hand washed and we did these once a week as well, and let the stuff dry on laundry racks in a remote part of the basement with a dehumidifier in the room.

Remember, at this time I was used to only having one or two clients each twenty-four hours. So there was plenty of time to clean, wash and help Ed with his work. But with each passing week there were more and more offers of business. In the subsequent weeks and months my assistant increased her time with me to four afternoons a week and I hired a receptionist who could take calls, give tours and do intake interviews. This would free me and my assistant to concentrate on sessions. Months later I expanded the operation even more.

I have two pleasant hours of sleep before a call wakes me up. Then I go out back for a smoke and just relax for a few minutes. Ed is taking a supper break and we chat. He says it might be best if on, say, two days a week we did not take tours or sessions and instead concentrated on renovating. Ed said a friend of his would come and do the roof on those days and this would leave us more time for clients. So we make some scheduling decisions. In fact this friend spent much time helping Ed. They were long time buddies and Ed told him what was going on and made it very worth the friend's while to assist him and me on those days that there were no appointments, so the renovations and improvements to the property were actually ahead of schedule. They were basically finished just a few months later, in the winter, so when Jerry went south for the winter Ed told him we would be finished by spring, while we were actually almost finished when he went.

At 6:30 I put on some makeup and my robe and sit down at my desk in the parlor. The dining area beside the kitchen is being worked on and in a couple of weeks I will move my desk and a couple of chairs in there along with a spanking bench and it will serve as the Headmistress's Office as well as my business office where calls would be taken, interviews conducted, notes and other paperwork done and punishment administered by the Headmistress. However, for now, all this was done in the living room, or parlor.

It's thirty minutes before the tour client arrives, and I decide to use the time to do some paperwork. I take out the files of the two clients who had sessions that day and note what we had done for them, what worked well and what didn't, what they said we should keep in mind for next time and so forth. As a rule I also make notes about whether we should go extra lengths with any clients, meaning whether it might be worth our while to do extra for them, either because they tipped us or we got the impression they were rich and could afford to spend a lot at our place. I also take care to note which clients were difficult to deal with because they demanded a lot for what they were paying in terms of effort, detail, and preparation, in which case it would be strictly by the book with them, meaning no extra time and no extra effort. Normally I make my notes at the end of the day, when it's quiet and the phone isn't ringing, but I learned the value of using down time wisely.

The 7:00 tour arrives right on time. I do the usual intake interview, take his $25 and show him the place. The look on his face is astonishing. It looks like he was experiencing a revelation. He says he can't believe a place like this exists. I don't believe him. I ask him if he had ever been to any of the houses downtown or visited a dominatrix before. He says he had never even heard the term dominatrix until he was more than fifty, and when I show him some of the trade magazines he said he did not even know such publications existed until recently. He says he lived a very conventional and happy life in the suburbs of Toronto, had never paid for sex or cheated on his wife, and had always kept his fantasies and desires hidden. He was too concerned with the welfare of his three children to do anything that might create any awkwardness for them. He was happy with his career, a conservative occupation he told me a bit about. He had hobbies and community interests and loved how his wife occupied a nice social position and also would never do anything to cause a problem for her.

I ask him, then, why he's here. He said his kids, except for one, were on their own now. He says he's only working at his small firm (which he owned) part time and so had times when he could sneak away. He said he had inherited money when his parents died and his wife did not watch his spending, so he had funds put away only he knew about. Above all, he said, he had been finding his fantasies becoming more and more prominent in his thoughts and the desire to act them out stronger.

I tell him that men like him are fortunate when they could afford to act them out, and do so with complete discretion, yet not let their fantasy role play damage their real lives. I tell him if he wanted a divorce, it should be because he and his wife had grown apart, not because he wants to role play. Neither she nor his kids need know about it. He should live for himself a bit now too, I tell him. He appreciated this advice. His role play was basically cross-dressing, without the schoolroom or corporal punishment or even humiliation. He was just in love with women's clothing. The idea of a total transformation into a woman, as I describe it, makes his jaw drop and his eyes water. I take him into the boudoir and show him what I want to put him into, and tell him he could arrange for extended time dressed in extensive women's wear like a corset, nylons, high heels, makeup, wig and dresses. For example, for a special rate, he could be dressed up in the morning and undressed in the evening. Of course he might want to explore other fantasy role play. We talk money and possible schedules and then I tell him to think about it and call so we could set things up.

No sooner had he driven away than the 8:00 client arrives. This is an overnight client. His script was to be put into a straight jacket and locked in a cell overnight. I could even have other clients in the dungeon while he was in the cell. When that happened I would put a mask on him so he wouldn't be recognized, and he knew not to speak so his voice would not be recognized either. I would wake him up very early the next morning and he would get a cab back to the subway and return home early in the morning to get ready for work. He would usually shower before coming to see me and did not need to shower after, so he was less work for me. He also liked it when my receptionist and assistant were available, but did not insist on it. When they were available they would go into the cell and torture him for a few minutes too, so it was no big deal.

When he arrived he would be sent downstairs and told to put his clothes in the jail cell. Then I would arrive in a medical coat carrying a straight jacket, a diaper and plastic pants. I would order him to lie down and diaper him and put the pants on. Then he would stand up and I would buckle him into the straight jacket. Then various things would happen. I might whip him as I ordered him about. I might tie his feet, spread apart, to the jail cell bars and tickle them mercilessly. I might pinch his thighs mercilessly, or kick him as he thrashed around helplessly. I would usually leave him in the cell until shortly before it was time for me to go to sleep and before leaving him tell him that if he was still in the straight jacket when I came back later he would be tortured again. Before I went to sleep I would usually torture him for a few minutes. Sometimes I would stay and laugh at him while he struggled to escape. Sometimes I would leave it a bit loose and surprise him by coming in when he had almost escaped, and refasten the clasps.

In the morning I would wake him up and torture him again and tell him I might keep him for the day and make an example of him. One time I did, with his consent, and he actually spent over twenty-four hours in the jacket. Sometimes he actually got out of it, but I learned how to apply it to make this impossible. He usually visited about once every two or three weeks and we had a special bulk discount deal, meaning he gave me a big lump sum up front and got several of these sessions at much less than if he paid as he went.

On this day, after I torture the client in the straight jacket for the last time I check to see that all paperwork was done and then have a bath and go to sleep. The phone is quiet for the night. It has been what was to become a typical day. I think as I fell asleep about a few weeks back, when it was not busy and the phone did not ring so much. I'm grateful now just to be able, sometimes, to kick back and relax, have naps, read, watch some television, have a good meal and maybe get out a bit. I always have mixed feelings when I'm busy and the money is coming in, as indeed I do when I am able to take it easy and little or no money is coming in. I just take it as it comes day by day, but I realize that this will not last forever and I know that when I have to leave there will be plenty of time to do other things and take a break from this work.

And that was this one day in the life of this one dominatrix.

CHAPTER 17

A Day in My Life:
Saturday, December 1, 2001

A Bit of History

In September 1994 I was raided in Thornhill and did not practice as a dominatrix again until 1998. I fought my legal battles, had my two hysterectomies and lived quietly. From 1998 until 2000 I acquired the use of a second house (which I ran until 2002), but this time in downtown Toronto. I rented it in stages. What I mean is that in 1998 I had the main floor and basement to live in and work from. In the next year or so I also took possession of the upper two floors, each as they became available.

The business grew and developed as this space opened up. At first I just had a little dungeon and a couple of rooms for cross-dressers. I did little advertising, and did not even have my Web site until 1999. Finally late in 2000 I had my Bondage Hotel, which occupied most of the top floor and the Sissy Maid Academy and Charm School, which basically occupied the third floor. Of course this meant I also had to have the money and then the time and also the help to furnish and stock the rooms.

Old clients, new clients, colleagues and friends were very helpful with donations of clothing, furniture, equipment, implements and their time. They were very anxious to see me in business again with a high profile. They wanted me to make a statement to the world as well as help me and my daughter, to whom many became dedicated in the best sense. They were as supportive as they could be. Some have died, the rest remain supportive.

Why I Picked This Day

There were many reasons. For one thing, in early December 2001, business was getting back to where it was just before the terrorist attacks of September. For many weeks following the tragedy there were very few visitors to my house from abroad.

Another reason was that Saturday itineraries normally, by now, made use of all the facility had to offer. This included the usual sessions with clients, a weekly class I was giving to aspiring doms, weekend overnight guests from abroad, a couple of hours for an open house for the media and in the evening our weekly Saturday night fetish party.

On this day my daughter, who I will call Janet, was still with me. In a few weeks she would be leaving for South America to live with her boyfriend at his family's home. They were planning to get married eventually. She worked full time as a dom with me right up until her departure.

Also at this time my receptionist from Thornhill, Judy, was back with me, basically full time. Ed, who helped me set up and run the Bondage Bungalow in Thornhill, was also now living at the house, acting as security and much else. I also had a retired American soldier, a cross-dresser, living with me as my personal slave. I called him Suzy Maid. He stayed with me when he was not working as a trucker. Another man, also a cross-dresser, acted as my personal slave most weekends, when he came in from just outside Toronto. He had a regular job during the week. I called him Cathy Maid. I also had the doms, who came and went during the day as their schedules required. So on this day I had my little army. I was going to need it.

Remember as well that at this time I did not yet know I was seriously ill, although I was having more and more days filled with fatigue, various aches and pains and nausea. It was not until months later, when I finally saw the doctor and had tests, that I found out I had advanced Hepatitis C, with an accompanying cirrhotic liver—among other diseases.

There was also the fact that I did not know, regardless of my health, that we would have to vacate the property in a few months because the owner became available to renovate the property. It was always an understanding we had, that when he was between assignments this would be done. The place needed it, and he was going to take a year off and get the property ready for the years to come. He did however promise to give me at least three months notice. He did so about two months after the day

I am telling you about, and let me move out a floor at a time over the next few months.

At the peak of the operation, and the day I am telling you about, we had four floors, with a total of about thirteen rooms. There was a large dungeon, fully equipped. There were rooms for cross-dressers, with racks of clothing and so forth. There was a clothing store up front. There was the room known as the Bondage Hotel with a massive four poster bed built for heavy bondage, which we used for sessions and where guests paid to stay. There was a lounge, two kitchens, three bathrooms, an office and a couple of rooms where we slept at night.

So all in all, the ingredients were in place this day for many interesting things to happen. This is the most interesting day I can recall, with the help of my papers and the recollections of some of those mentioned above, from when I ran my Toronto house.

Saturday December 1, 2001

8:15: Janet wakes me up. We have this arrangement that whoever gets up first makes a point of waking up the other at eight. She loves to sleep and both she and I set alarms to ensure we are up, showered, dressed and ready to do business by nine. I have a tough time getting up today. I seem to be getting more and more tired and sore with each passing month. It occurs to me again that I should see a doctor and get some tests done. It also occurs to me that I am afraid of what the doctor may tell me, and may be better off not knowing.

*   *   *

8:30: I'm in the shower. I take my time, get dried and get dressed in casual clothing. While in the shower I go over what lies ahead of me today. We have to give breakfast to a couple who were staying in the Bondage Hotel. After we secure their belongings in a locked cupboard they will head out for the day, and return for a session with me and a couple of other doms before supper. This means we can use the Bondage Hotel for sessions and show it to the media. They will go out for dinner for a few hours and then return and join our fetish party. They are paying many hundreds of dollars for their two days, so we give them every attention, despite all else that will be going on in the house today.

*   *   *

8:45: Ed had made coffee. I help Ed and Janet prepare a breakfast of eggs, bacon, toast and hash browns. Suzy Maid cooks when she is there. She was a cook in the army. If not, Ed cooks. Whoever is there eats at 9:00. Today Janet, Ed, Cathy Maid, Suzy and I are there for breakfast. Judy will arrive later. Suzy slept in the locked coffin and Cathy Maid slept in the nursery, chained into the crib.

*   *   *

9:00: As we eat we go over the day's itinerary. Judy had left it before she left last night. She usually arrives late in the afternoon and leaves late at night. In addition to tending to the events and clients and students and so forth there were the basic maintenance chores and errands. Every day the house has to be cleaned from top to bottom. I make my usual round of the entire house to see what has to be done. Laundry was always done Saturday mornings, with Ed and Janet going to the Laundromat. I don't like to send out Suzy Maid or Cathy Maid, because they like to assume their slave personas when staying at the house, and they never look normal when they do that. The floors have to be washed and vacuumed. This chore was usually split between Ed, Janet and me. We are going to do it before they head out to the Laundromat. Ed was a good worker. Janet, on the other hand preferred to just order the "maids" around. For some reason, as my daughter, she felt entitled. This annoyed me greatly as I am the Madame. I was upset at my daughter at lot, it seems. Although it pains me to say so she was basically an adult brat back then. But I knew she was leaving in a few weeks. I might never see her again. I knew she would not likely be able to live like that where she was headed to. I let it go.

*   *   *

9:30: I'm in my office. I check appointments and files and make sure all of that stuff is ready for the day. I call some of the doms to see who was coming in for the media event and fetish party, and who was available for any sessions that may be booked. Then I go to visit the couple staying in the Bondage Hotel upstairs. I put on some high boots and leather gloves and a leather coat, take my riding crop and head upstairs. Part of what they wanted was a brief scene in the morning. This involved the wife as a submissive. The husband would hold her down while I applied restraints so she was spread eagled and naked in the bondage bed. Then I handcuff the husband to a corner of the bed and tickle her mercilessly for about ten minutes while he watched helplessly and begs me to stop. Then I let him go. I leave. She is at his mercy. I hear her screaming as I make my way downstairs. They knew to be ready to go within an hour. They have sightseeing to do.

* * *

10:00: I am cleaning where the maids had already cleaned because they required constant supervision. They would use rags in the kitchen that had just been used to clean the bathroom. I found this extremely upsetting. After I finished inspecting and redoing some cleaning I go to the dressing parlor to tidy up the clothes in preparation for client visits scheduled that day. I then give final cleaning instructions to all concerned, and Janet and Ed head to the Laundromat. I told them that the place must be ready for the media visit, and also that everyone must be in full costume.

* * *

10:15: A few minutes of quiet. I have decided to offer sessions at the usual rate for clients who like to be exhibited. The media can take pictures of them and so I get advertising and client revenue at the same time. They will get long sessions for the short session rate. I tell them they will be disguised. I call some of them and one agrees. Another agrees, but says he cannot afford it now, so I tell him he can pay in future, provided he tells no one. Then I tell a couple of supporters who can be relied on to volunteer when needed that they are indeed needed. I spoke to them earlier in the week. I tell them they can stay for the party as well. I tell them all to arrive at 1:30 so they can be prepped for the cameras and reporters. I tell them they are not to speak to the reporters during the visit or agree to an interview after.

* * *

10:30: I go up to the Bondage Hotel again and spend a few minutes chatting with my guests. I take the woman aside and whisper to her that at their afternoon session she gets revenge on her husband for taking advantage of her when I left her helpless and at his mercy this morning. We put their stuff securely away so the visitors won't see it and I take any valuables they won't have with them to be lock away in a secured part of the house that is inaccessible to the visitors. I remind them that the room will be used for demonstration purposes when they are gone. They have no problem with that and I wish them a happy day. Back down the stairs to the cross-dressing area.

* * *

10:45: I check in with the maids. We are ahead of schedule. I tell them to let in the clients coming in around 1:30 and to try to get some rest. It is going to be a very busy day. I tell them to also be ready to help Janet and Ed when they get back with the laundry in about an hour. Then I do yet another tour of the entire house to ensure everything is in order. Ed will give the Bondage Hotel a thorough cleaning and make sure everything is in place when he is back in any event. Fortunately, everything seems to be in good order.

* * *

11:45: It has been a quiet hour. I have a cigarette and some more coffee and I answer a few routine phone calls. I book a client for a session just before the fetish night is to begin. He asks for heavy bondage and discipline. I have had him before. He likes to be tortured and then go to some fancy event or other and look at all the well dressed superior women and what not. He says he feels very smug, because anything he might fantasize about doing with them he has just done and he says it's a great secret to have. In the past he has actually arrived in a tuxedo. He is a divorced executive with no children. He is scheduled to come at six and will be fashionably late for a posh reception at about 7:30.

* * *

12:00: The phone is the lifeline of this place. It is more important than anything else, although I should tell you that whenever I talk about the phones here I am also referring to the Internet. That is true even for "phone sessions". A caller charges about fifty dollars plus taxes to his credit card to speak for thirty minutes to, say, a dom. On-line sessions are just starting up too. I am an expert at domination over the phone, Judy is close and Janet can also do a reasonable job. The phone or Internet is also where we answer enquiries and book appointments. Today, for example, confirmations and enquiries about our evening fetish party make up some of the calls. Others call to book regular appointments or stays at the Bondage Hotel or the Sissy Maid Academy. Today there are calls about the Open House I arranged for the media. And lest we forget, there is the usual complement of "prank calls". On a day like today, which is an exceptional day, the phone rings constantly. We sometimes say "Someone get the cash register". It is important not to miss a call and to respond to e-mails quickly and carefully.

* * *

12:30: Ed and Janet are back. The maids have been helping each other get dressed and Janet and I come to be dressed by them. I am helped into a large black corset, intricately laced. I am helped into nylons which attach by garters that I can't reach and then into high heeled thigh high boots and long black leather gloves. Janet and I put each other's makeup on. Then I leave to oversee further preparations while Janet is helped into a tight latex dress and black boots. She is much more mobile than I am, but then she, like so many of the other doms, like most of the young and trim ones, does not need much fetish clothing to look dominant. They can look like women warriors and so forth with relatively little effort. For us older and heavier gals it takes more preparation.

* * *

12:45: I welcome a couple of the participants for our 1:00 class. Then a couple more arrive. I tell them that this class is different than most and that I will be giving them the option of some limited hands-on experience because of the media day. The class today will just be a short lecture and I will take a few quick questions. Janet and Ed brought some finger food which the gals will eat in the classroom while I gave the class. Six gals come to the class today. Two are novices who come out of curiosity. I ask them either to leave before the media arrive or if they stay, to just observe. The other four have been to the class before and are here to day to learn a bit and help out with the Open House and are invited to attend the fetish party in the evening. During the Open House they can have their faces disguised if they wish. All six are there by 1:00. The two novices, who came together, say they are unable to stay for the Open House.

* * *

1:00: I begin my lecture. I talk about how to deal with the media, since this is obviously very topical today. I tell the four who will stay for the Open House that they will each be at a "post" the entire two hours, meaning they will be beside a restraint device to which a client or volunteer will be fastened, or supervise a client in a straightjacket. When our media guests arrive, the gals and subs will follow a script (more about that later). Otherwise they just stand there. We arrange what each will wear. Janet gives each of them a quick makeover before the media is due. One of the four comes ready with a vinyl cat-suit she owns.

* * *

1:15: The maids watch the store downstairs (which is open for business) and other posts, such as the door, while I do a quick go around and check in with Judy, who came in early today to ensure phone coverage. Basically she will handle the phones alone, but earlier this morning, I asked one of my experienced doms to help Judy with the phones. This means that if a request comes in for a thirty minute session Judy can do it and the incoming calls are not missed. Both gals are compensated for their time, which are only a few hours. Janet is preparing the gals from the class who are staying. They tell her it must be amazing to do this for a living and have me as a mother.

* * *

1:30: One by one the clients or supporters who are to be submissives during the Open House arrive and one at a time, as their doms are ready,

I take them and their dom to their "post". I try to match the client or supporter with their preferences, but do not let them choose which dom. One pair is at the spanking bench. The sub is chained to it and is naked face down. When the reporters are present the dom whips him. I give her permission to only use a basic light stroke and tell him to say "Thank you Mistress, another please" each time, but to also whimper as he says it. Another sub is in the swing, meaning he is hanging spread-eagled from the ceiling. The dom is to tickle his armpits and feet when the media is there and laugh and tell him he needs more as she tickles him. The other sub is in a cage, with his arms suspended above his head and feet chained to the floor. The dom pokes him with a stick while he squirms to protect himself. The other finally arrives and is chained to the four posters of the bondage bed in the Bondage Hotel, with the dom straddling him while she tickles and slaps him whenever the reporters are there or within hearing range. All the subs are wearing masks, whether they want to or not. I don't want someone being identified as a client of mine in the media.

* * *

1:45: The first reporters arrive, thinking they are being sneaky by being early and supposedly catching me unprepared or putting me in a position where I have to make them wait. No such luck for them. The maid at the door, when he is told who they are, sends them to my office. He introduces them with the words "Reporters Headmistress." I do my fiendish laugh and have them sit down and I gave a brief interview before taking them on a tour. I tell them pictures are fine and that those who do not want their faces in the media can be masked or, like Janet, wear heavy glasses and a wig that makes them look entirely different than they normal selves.

* * *

2:00: The first tour. All doms and subs perform well. The reporter and photographer that came with her love it. I ask a couple of the doms whether we should let these media people go or keep them here for punishment and of course they say, according to script, that my whims, cruelties and moods should determine their fate. I say I will punish them some other day. They love this theater and the visuals and the shots they get and I show them the rest of the place and then the door and thank them for coming. A couple of the photos and stories will be printed in the papers (nationwide, as it turns out). One of the reports that will air on television is a video with me showing them around. I should mention that I have one open house per year as part of my advertising strategy.

*   *   *

3:00: In quick succession the last two of the three media parties show up. They get the same go around as the first two and are gone. Then I go downstairs and tell the doms to release the subs and tell the four doms and three of the subs to leave if they wish, or hang around or return later for the fetish party. By 3:30 the six of the eight are gone. A few will return for the party in a few hours. One of the gals said she was going to the library to do homework in the interim. One of the gals goes back to the dungeon to supervise and perhaps lightly torment and humiliate the client who was still in the dungeon, chained to the spanking horse, his buttocks presented in the air for punishment.

*   *   *

3:30: Ed tells Janet and me that we can come up for a drink or a bite and we do. I tell the maids they can rest for a while but they should make sure everything is spotless. After a bite Janet and I check over the Bondage Hotel. The couple is to come back soon for a session and we don't want anything out of place. We change the sheets on the bed and put the restraints and chains where they belong and put on a night light before leaving. Janet and I remain in our outfits because we will be doing a session with them in about an hour. I go across the top floor and check in with Judy and her assistant in the office. Everything seems under control. I go to the bathroom and then lie down for a nap. Ed helps me lie down. I am almost immobilized in my corset and boots and it is almost impossible for me to get down and up on my own, yet too much trouble to undo me and do me back up again. Oh, what we women go through! I fall asleep.

*   *   *

4:00: While I sleep the phones have been ringing and things are getting nicely set up for the fetish party. The client coming for his pre-function torture calls to confirm but said he might need to come at 5:30. He did not say whether he would be in a tuxedo. But if he comes in one, he won't be in it for long.

*   *   *

4:30: The couple who rented the Bondage Hotel returns. Janet quickly wakes me up and then puts her fright wig on and gets some handcuffs. Then she lets them in and when they are upstairs she tackles the husband and cuffs his hands behind his back. She then tells him that his wife has lured him into a trap and she gets a full leather hood that provides complete sensory deprivation except for breathing. She puts it on and locks it and removes the handcuffs, but the husband cannot move without hurting himself so Janet tells the wife to remove his clothes while she holds him down.

*   *   *

4:45: Now he is chained to the four corners of the heavy bondage bed and is completely naked and vulnerable. Janet comes to get me and I proceed upstairs. Man, do I ever feel better after that nap! Remember, I am in my full dominatrix outfit: corset, boots, etc. I order them to remove the hood and when he sees me he looks terrified. Janet also looks menacing. She also knows how to make a facial expression that makes her look really pissed off. I ask the wife if we may punish him for what he did to her earlier. She says laughingly that we may. We do. We tickle him and laugh loud while we do it. We hand a feather to her and she tickles his feet, while he begs for mercy. She says if she stops the Headmistress and her assistant will start. It's his choice.

*   *   *

5:00: It seems he has had about all he can take, if the fact that he's crying uncontrollably is any indication. I order Janet to leave, and she does. I then tell the wife that he's hers to do with as she wishes, but there will be an extra fee if we have to bury or cremate him. She laughs as I leave. Then just as I close the door Janet reminds me that one of the clients, the one who paid and who posed during the media session, was still in bondage on the spanking bench and was owed a very severe flogging. She had checked on him and his dom about an hour ago and told them the Headmistress is preparing for his punishment. The two of us make our way down three flights of stairs into the dungeon. There he is, still with his apprentice dom watching over him. He is telling her about some job hunting tips or something like that. I scream at him for being too friendly and tell the dom she has done a good job gaining his confidence and pretending to be friendly. Now it is time for him to suffer.

* * *

5:15: Janet and I have been applying the lashes and cane and screaming laughter these last several minutes. We have not even bothered to try to communicate with the client, but he knows the safety words and so forth. He is an ardent submissive, into very heavy punishment and prolonged bondage. By the end of the evening party, for which he is also staying, he will have been here for almost twelve hours, paid us a couple of hundred dollars and helped us with our advertising and in training a possible new dom. He likes us to leave marks that take a couple of weeks to heal. They are his trophies. He is not disappointed. Then we tell him we are now ready to start his punishment of five hundred lashes. Janet gags him. He thinks he is finished. The apprentice dom starts to look a bit scared. I just wink at her and we leave the room and take her with us and tell her we are just scaring him. We tell her she can go back in and remove his restraints and let him go. She can leave with him if that was what they were talking about but that they should be back for the fetish party by eight. It is turning out to be a banner day for him.

* * *

5:30: Mr. Possible Tuxedo arrives. No tuxedo, but a very nice suit. Janet and I greet him. He has a routine. He likes to be watched and shouted at as he undresses and then we quickly restrain him over a whipping bench and both whip him at the same time. This requires us to concentrate. Then, while one of us strikes from behind where he cannot see, the other is in front of him screaming abuse. The words are important, words to the effect that he will be late for his function or that one of the well dressed society women who will be there (we don't tell him which one) is watching on a camera now and will bring him here after for more punishment which she will administer.

* * *

6:30: Mr. No Tuxedo is gone. Why is it so quiet all of a sudden? Never mind, just enjoy it. I have a light bite upstairs and a cigarette after. I want to get out of the corset and boots, but I'm afraid that if they come off I might not be able to stand getting into them again. I can't resist. I summon Cathy Maid and he helps me undress and we go down to the dungeon with me wearing nothing but a bathrobe. I lie down on one of the torture tables and he rubs me for about half an hour. He is trained by me to know what kind of massages I like and don't like. The only condition is that he is tortured and humiliated in return for the privilege of massaging the Headmistress. I fall asleep as I am being rubbed.

* * *

7:00: Unknown to me Judy booked another client for 7:30. He wants a one hour session with Janet and Contessa Cintra, our fabulous blond glamazon dom. He likes to be interrogated and made to confess his sins. He is a regular, who visits about once a month and likes the two doms to dress as policewomen. Cintra arrives just before the session and changes into her "uniform", a one piece black suit, not leather. She wears long black boots and fishnet stockings and black gloves. Janet has on her outfit from earlier in the day and they go down to the dungeon. I did not know about this until I saw him at the fetish party. Cintra and Janet keep on their outfits for the fetish party. They come down to the dungeon, wake me and I go back to the top floor.

* * *

7:30: Cathy Maid helps me back into my corset, nylons and thigh high bitch boots. The other maids and dom students have been watching television and having a bite to eat. The maids wait on the gals who are not in session. These men have a limitless appetite for being slaves to these girls or me. I come down to the floor below the top one and sit with them a bit. My daughter will be leaving so many friends she has made behind when she leaves Canada in a few weeks. Janet and Cintra are in the dungeon with a client. I'm glad that we are doing the extra business. I hear them screaming at him and hear the blows being struck and him crying for mercy and them laughing at his helpless struggles. No need to join them. Routine.

* * *

8:00: The fetish party guests start arriving. The couple from the Bondage Hotel come down and join us. The maids serve us drinks and food and I introduce the itinerary for the evening. I tell them we will wait to begin until Janet and Cintra join us. There are six guests, not including the couple. There are three apprentice doms, two maids, myself and soon Janet and Cintra. When they arrive the games will begin. Ed is upstairs watching the hockey game, but listening on the baby monitor in case any security is needed. Not likely.

* * *

8:15: I notice the wife of the couple is a bit disconcerted as her husband is surrounded by the doms and she does not appear to be comfortable being with the two men dressed as sissy maids. I begin by saying that I will, when the whim strikes me, order a particular dom to spank a particular guest. Dinner is served as I speak. We will begin by playing a game of musical chairs, where the last sub to sit down is spanked by all doms present. We would then play Spin the Dial, which is a simple board game which lists twelve punishments. Client names were put in a hat and when one is chosen he will spin the wheel. When it stops all the doms fall upon him, restrain him and do what the spin indicates, if anything. For example, it might say the client has to worship a dom with other doms whacking him if he is lost for words, or they might hold him down and tickle him, or pinch him, or spank him or whatever the spin says to do. We have restraints and a few striking implements, but little else. The clients love this. They love it when the doms fight with each other to see who will inflict his punishment. One of the favorites is the spin called "bondage contest". In this case a second name is drawn and two doms tie up one sub each and the last one to escape, if either of them are able, are punished by the dom who tied the other one up. Perhaps most of the clients who are here love seeing all these doms in costume. They have every excuse to stare at them and they are in a virtual heaven for a fetishist.

* * *

8:30: The games begin. The husband and wife do not want to participate, just watch. After about an hour they leave and I go with them to the Bondage Hotel upstairs and restrain the wife to the bed. I laugh loudly and fiendishly, say goodnight and head back to the party.

* * *

8:45: I get back to the party just as Cintra and Janet join in. Their client did not want to stay. He was worried about being recognized. They continue to play spin the dial.

* * *

9:30: We all head down to the dungeon. It is important that food is digested and that the clients and guests did not eat too much, given what is to come. We watch them carefully for this and do a bit of an intake interview about limits and health conditions if they are new clients or just guests. In the dungeon all clients are restrained in various ways. One is put in the swing naked. Another fastened to the spanking bench. Another is put in the stocks. Another is put in a straightjacket on a soft mat. A fifth is tied spread eagled on a restraint table. The sixth guest does not want to participate and leaves, because, he says, he has to be up very early the next morning and did not realize how late it would get if he stayed. Then the final game begins. It is called Interrogation. Each dom has one restrained sub to work on and begins tickling him. The sub who calls for a stop first is declared the loser and all doms set upon him for a while. Then the remaining four each have their dom work on them again, but this time with pinching. Again, the loser is made to suffer even more. The gals love this game. They make sure that each round doesn't last too long. The last one to submit is released and can just watch, as another round begins with the remaining four subs.

* * *

10:30: Before the guests leave we offer them sessions for an extra charge and they can choose which dom will punish them and how. If it is one of the apprentices we insist that it be supervised by me, Janet or Cintra. A couple of them agree to an extra session. The others are released and seen to the door by the maids. The two who stay are tortured at the same time and can see each other's sessions as they have their own. This is very arousing for some clients. One of them wants to be whipped by a few doms at the same time, and this is done. Since we are all there for the party we do not charge the extra fees we normally would if each of us had to be there specifically for the session.

*   *   *

12:30: All guests and clients are gone. Janet and the other gals change and leave. Some of them want to dance and party at an all night bar. A couple of them go home. I check in with the maids and tell them to begin cleaning up, but if they are tired they may get out of their high heels and so forth and go to sleep. I check in with Ed and say goodnight and then Judy and I go over the day's finances and what is booked for tomorrow. Judy helped me undress. Heaven! Nothing beats getting out of that corset and those boots. Then I run a hot bath and get in.

*   *   *

1:00: I lie here in the hot bath and think of how quickly the day has gone. We did good business today. The fetish party guests have brought in revenue of almost a thousand dollars when the extra sessions are included. We had good publicity from the media. I did some training and gave some exposure to potential new doms. We did another thousand dollars of business from clients and over the phones. Finally, we have the Bondage Hotel couple who would leave tomorrow afternoon. They paid well over a thousand dollars for their visit. It was a good day, business-wise.

*   *   *

1:30: I am in bed. As I drift off to sleep I reflect that I have what I wanted. I am queen of my castle. My daughter is with me, but I am of course worried about what is to become of her. I have a roof over my head and

174

food and am warm in the winter. There was a time when even these things were denied me. But in my heart I know that my visits to the doctor loom. What will happen when we have to leave this place? I look forward to tomorrow. It should be a quiet day, a Sunday, with maybe a few sessions and a bit of administration and putting the place in order and seeing off the couple in the Bondage Hotel. I fall asleep dreaming of a day off.

And that was this one day in the life of this one dominatrix.

CHAPTER 18

Interesting Questions

Over the last few years I have been encouraged to post blogs on my Web site and through social media to share my thoughts and answer questions. Most of the postings concerned the legal battles and issues related to it. As I said earlier, in this book I am not discussing legal, social or political issues. However, some interesting questions of a personal nature, or relating to the dominatrix lifestyle, came along which I did not raise in my first book. So, in no particular order, let me share some of those thoughts with you again now.

* * *

How does it feel to have had your life made public these last fifteen or so years?

Today it feels good. I feel validated. Also, I have a book for sale and publicity helps sales. At first it was a bit embarrassing and I worried about confrontations, but gradually I accepted that my life would become an open book, especially when I signed on for the constitutional challenge.

Of course it bothered me a bit when the media got the facts wrong or said negative things about me, but now I expect that sometimes. Today it is actually a constant source of interest to me to see how the media is so often inaccurate, or otherwise misrepresents matters, whether it is about me or the issues in my legal battles. I have been able to set the record straight in my first book. I don't expect fairness in return, and I know that the opinions people have of me and what I have stood for will always vary.

* * *

What happens when strangers recognize you in public?

Most of the time I am not recognized. I am good at disguising myself, and I don't go out that often, but sometimes there are interesting encounters. Most of the time we are both shocked. A few months ago I went to a supermarket. A woman came up to me and said "Are you Terri-Jean Bedford?" Although I was in my "disguise" I told her I was. She told me she had always wanted to meet me and asked me for my autograph, which I gave her, on back of a flyer she found. We had a nice chat and she told me to keep up the fight and stand up for women victims of our laws. Another time two guys saw me sitting on a park bench and yelled "How much?" A few times I have actually been asked for autographs. Many times people have come up to me and said they were pleased to meet me or have said how much they supported what I was doing (usually referring to the legal battle against the so called prostitution laws). People often stare but do so only briefly and say nothing. Overall, considering how much I change my appearance when I go out, I am surprised at how many people appear to recognize me. Such is the power of images in the media in our lives. Thank goodness they are almost always friendly.

* * *

How did being a dominatrix change you?

It was very different from my personal experience as a prostitute selling sex. For the first half of my life my struggles were often for mere survival. I sometimes had to steal to eat. I had to sell my body in the most dangerous ways possible. I was so down and out and desperate most of the time that the only people I could associate with were those on the margins and things like drug and alcohol abuse, which got them there, rubbed off on me. I was always just responding to the needs of the day and mistakes of the days before. I was almost always in over my head, sometimes from poor judgment, sometimes from desperation.

It was different for me when I was a dominatrix running my houses. I was very business-like and practical and dealing with more well-heeled men and women in more elegant settings that made me feel and act more

177

professional and lady-like. I enjoyed what I was doing and it showed in how I felt and acted. Sometimes I still had pressures, but they were more like the pressures of someone with a challenging business to run or a creative artist under numerous pressures. My time as a dominatrix and the behavior of the authorities in my cases also brought me many allies. So, being a dominatrix changed me most, I would say, in that I did not feel I was alone in facing the world. But then again, this is my personal experience.

I suspect that when you ask me this question you may be thinking about what having helpless men at my mercy and torturing or humiliating them did to my personality. I think it improved it. It did wonders for my ego and confidence to have powerful yet helpless men begging me to punish them, or stop punishing them, and worshipping at my feet.

*   *   *

How do you like not being a dominatrix?

I don't. I still practice my trade in a very limited capacity, never for money, among a close inner circle only. If I was healthy, and was funded to the point that I did not have to make ends meet, I would have no problem with reopening. I do miss doing sessions. However, when your health is as bad as mine, with my failing liver, spinal stenosis and fibromyalgia, you don't feel a big desire to take on responsibilities. I can't even be depended on to make sessions if I booked them. Some days I am bedridden. I only go out when I am feeling relatively well, or when the matter is of great importance. So, as you can see, there are everyday things I miss more than being a dominatrix.

*   *   *

Which dominatrix roles did you like most and least?

Every dominatrix enjoys some things about her job more than others. Obviously we like the pure dominatrix stuff more than the administrative aspects of the job, such as cleaning, paperwork and answering phones. First of all, longer scenes were better. I was always frustrated, as was the client, when the hour went by so quickly. For example, a cross-dresser would take off his clothes, I would help him into restrictive female attire, and there might only be a bit more than enough time of his hour left to get him changed again. Role play can be greatly enhanced when prolonged. Secondly, I would say, honestly, that there were many role-play scenarios I enjoyed above the others, but at that I will stop. Some things are best kept secret. Sorry. It would be like a magician giving away the secrets of doing the magic tricks, and some clients I had might be disappointed in what I say.

*   *   *

Where should a dominatrix operate from?

It depends on what scenes she wishes to do. If it is simple basic bondage and discipline she can do outcalls and bring a bag or suitcase with what she needs, and dress, perhaps under an overcoat, as required. If she does, say, medical or cross-dresser scenes, then she obviously needs a place of her own to keep all the stuff, or she has to rent such a place or be employed by such a place. Some doms have cottages which are fully equipped. Some have bachelor apartments they rent solely for their business appointments, with the equipment locked up ready for deployment on short notice. So it depends on how much capital she has and overhead she can cope with. I think the idea of the bachelor apartment I described is best of all for a couple of gals just starting out. It is inexpensive, can be shared by more than one dom, can be easily replaced if for some reason it has to close and can be downtown where the businessmen are. They can also, on a part time basis, work in the upper end houses, so as to have that experience as well. Overall, looking back, I would say the key is to be able to make and save money each week, if you don't have money or a big backer at the start.

*   *   *

Where did you get your clothes and equipment?

I got my wardrobe in many ways. Some items had to be bought from fetish clothing stores at a high price, the obvious examples would be thigh high bitch boots with stiletto heels and long black leather gloves. Some items could be bought at second hand shops or yard sales, like leather coats, leather skirts and women's shoes. Some items were bought from middle range retail outlets, like bras, girdles, corsets, stockings and the like. I went to drug stores for most makeup and false eyelashes. For wigs I went to specialty wig stores. Some of my wardrobe was sold to me second hand by doms going out of business, or loaned to me by them when for one reason or another they had too much inventory. Some doms who worked for me had their own wardrobes. Finally, some clients would bring in their own clothes for cross-dressing or buy me or my doms gifts of clothing they wanted to see us in.

The same variety of sources applied to my equipment, but I had a couple of clients, S&M enthusiasts, who were also carpenters and renovators. They built a jail cell and some devices clients could be fastened to, and helped construct my dungeons and did other renovations and repairs in return for sessions. Things like chains and fasteners I got at hardware stores. I bought some school desks and blackboards at an auction. Clients also brought me restraints, harnesses and straightjackets they may have owned or bought for me as gifts from the fetish stores in downtown Toronto. However I personally selected my whips, paddles and specialty bondage masks from the best high end fetish outlets.

*   *   *

Was it comfortable to dress as a dominatrix? Did you enjoy it?

You can't always be comfortable when you make yourself attractive because you are turned out for the occasion, and not according to how you are feeling at the time. That aside, wearing the tight clothing, such as a corset we were expected to wear, the boots, gloves and so forth was not comfortable, but most of us loved getting dressed up. We loved the look on the men's faces when they saw us, how their jaws would drop, eyes widen and mouths go dry. We loved the feeling of empowerment that comes from being worshipped simply because of how we looked. Very few women can enjoy this based on their natural looks.

*   *   *

Did you feel safe running your houses?

You bet I did. I had male security there almost all the time. Even when they were not present I felt safer than working the streets or as an escort. I even felt safer than most women feel in their offices, where men sexually harass them so often, or on dates where so many are raped, not to mention being assaulted walking the streets or in home invasions. Few of these incidents are even reported. Only about ten per cent of rapes, I have read, are reported. I never felt safer in my life. Having men helpless and at my mercy certainly didn't make me feel less safe either.

*   *   *

How has your family felt about your dominatrix career and your legal challenge to the laws against prostitution?

My natural mother and father died when I was only a few years old. My first step father died when I was young as well. My foster mother was a religious woman and when my houses in Windsor and Thornhill were raided she was appalled. She thought what I was doing was sinful. She could not for the life of her understand why men would pay me to do what I did to them. I was an embarrassment to her. Her husband said little to me about what I did. He let her do the talking, but I don't think he was as critical. My foster mother died many years ago. I wonder what she would say now.

My natural sisters have tended to avoid me but I don't know whether it is because of what I do or just the usual awkwardness of staying in touch when in different cities. My step brothers and my sister in law, who live in another province, say they are supportive of my legal battles, but pretty much have avoided saying anything much to me about whether they like or dislike what I have done for a living. I have not asked them for their opinions. It's none of my business.

My daughter is my biggest supporter. I have trained her as a dominatrix and she may pursue this path in the future in some manner. She has no time for anyone who says I have done or am doing anything wrong. My grandson is too young to make much of all this, but he loves showing me pictures of myself in the paper. His biggest criticism of me is that I make him do homework, read and restrict his video game time when I baby-sit.

* * *

In your first book you spoke about your daughter extensively. How do you get along with her now?

As I've said she is my biggest supporter. We may even be doing a reality series for television together. I expect viewers will see that she still rebels when we are together. She has never fully forgiven me for not giving her a more stable home to grow up in or for leaving her in foster care. However as she gets older she sees more of what life is about and she realizes that I had none of the many supports she has as a single mother. She does not like being told by her mother what to do, what to wear, who to see and so forth. I think we get along fairly well, but we could do better.

* * *

What did being a dominatrix do to your sex drive?

Strange as it may sound, I am not sure. For one thing, I had two partial hysterectomies. Both were before I ran my last house in Toronto. So I had them when I was in my late thirties. Before that, when I ran my earlier houses, I did enjoy sex and had numerous boyfriends. But when I was a dominatrix I was simply too busy and too tired to be concerned about meeting guys.

There were times, brief times, when I was neither a sex worker nor a dominatrix. When I worked in offices I found I enjoyed meeting men and sometimes sleeping with them in my off hours. When I did manual work, I was usually too tired to care about sex. During those times I was also using drugs, so that too blunted my sex drive. So I guess that it was all the other things, mainly the pressures, not just being in leather and whipping men and so forth, that impacted on my sex drive. I really don't know if, absent the pressures, how being a dominatrix would have impacted on my sex drive.

* * *

What are your appearance tips for women?

It depends on what you are appearing for. Do you want men to whistle at you? Are you a professional woman in a conservative business office who wants to get ahead? Are you a secretary in that office who wants to seduce the men who work there? Are you a dominatrix in practice? Are you a housewife at a PTA meeting? Are you getting yourself ready for church?

So the first and most important thing is to recognize that certain looks work better in certain situations. But let's say that we are talking about basic attractiveness, not becoming glamorously beautiful, in most of the situations I listed above. I would say the second thing is to never trust your own judgment. Get both women and men to advise you on how to change your appearance for any of these given situations. I have seen television shows where they transform women's appearances, and it is amazing how much transforming they do. Next, accept that you can never feel comfortable with what works best. It is for the comfort of others. That is a price you pay. Then accept that like every other form of success there is hard work. Accept as well that it is not cheap.

Now that I have said all that I will give a few quick tips. Women spend too much time worrying about their weight. A woman's hair is half her beauty. Invest time and money in that and get the best advice you can. Visit the hairdresser every two weeks. Maintain in between. Next, a woman in a dress, showing her legs, is a different woman than one in pants. Women who say they are attractive in pant suits are wrong. Next to hair, legs make the woman. Men love women's feet. A woman in high heels is a different woman than when she is wearing low heels. Wear leather boots where appropriate. They drive men wild, so be selective about when you wear them. It's bad for your back, but there you are. Wear nylons or attractive stockings as much as possible. Finally, make sure your clothes fit well, and wear a girdle if it makes a noticeable improvement in your figure. Spend lots on tailoring. Wear makeup. Take makeup courses (not just one).

Finally, note I say finally, you may want to work on your weight. I say finally because our figures are hard to control, whereas the other things I mentioned can be done in a day, or thereabouts. Do not worry about your weight until you have addressed all the other things. In fact, you will feel better if you look better and will eat less and better. I do believe in exercise and good nutrition, but you asked me how to become more attractive.

Young women in jeans and shorts and spandex are attractive, but even they should consider what I have said above. The key is to remember that most men have fetishes and are attracted by a woman well turned out, almost regardless of her natural beauty.

*　　*　　*

What makes the perfect partner for you, or for any woman?

Let's start with me. When I was young I liked them big and tough, like bikers and so on. Today, I like them short, fat, bald and rich. But that is only from a dating perspective. I think if I was to get married, if that's what you mean by partner, I would want a balanced person: meaning one who is financially secure if not rich, mature but not too old, healthy, with many interests and who is a good listener and tolerant of differences in others. That's a long list and not very glamorous or exciting, but you have to remember that I am now in my fifties and am in poor health.

This brings me back to your question as it relates not only to me. That in turn brings me to a very, perhaps sad, truth, or truths, that women have a great deal of difficulty facing. For one thing, women will want different things from the man in their life. They want him to be sexually attracted to her forever. They want him to be a good provider. They want him to be a good son and son-in-law. They want him to be a respected member of the community. They want him to be a good father. They want him to be handsome. They want him to be tall.

How many men are any of those things for any length of time, if at all? Now let me add something else girls. He has his list too, and let me add to that that men generally are not in love with women, in the fullest sense, for more than a few years, if that. They are conditioned to be promiscuous.

The perfect partner, for both sexes, is a moving target. If you want a good father for your children, you will have to forgo almost all the other things on the list. If you don't want children, you might want to consider changing partners frequently. When you get older, you may find men your age dying or chasing younger women, and you may settle for even less.

So I guess to conclude, if I can conclude anything, I consider the perfect partner, for say permanent marriage, one who is comfortable with who we are and who we will become and who will not make the mistake of expecting too much from us.

*   *   *

How do you feel about being black, and how did that factor into your role as a dominatrix?

It is a disadvantage to be a person of color, even today, even in a cosmopolitan city like Toronto. Many members of other minority groups, let alone whites, look down on black people. One of the reasons I became a dominatrix was that clients generally preferred white women for sex and some would not pay a black woman for sex.

Now for me personally the experience of being a black woman is somewhat unusual. For one thing, I am only a very light brown. Many people seeing me, even without makeup and so forth think I am just tanned. My mother was a white woman, my father black. This explains why I am sometimes mistaken for a white woman. The net effect is that I have been treated better by the world than if I was darker, and this extended to when I was a dominatrix and to today when I am photographed during my legal battle appearances and so on. That is the reality, and it is sad the world is like that.

*   *   *

Did you ever fall in love with a client when you were a dominatrix? Did you tell him? What type of clients were you most attracted to personally?

I never fell in love with a client. Our contact was too fleeting and I had to keep focused. I had a business to run. Of course I found some clients charming and some attractive, but I never got to know any but a few well enough to have any chance of being seriously attracted to them. The ones I liked most, as I look back, were the short, fat and bald older clients. They seemed so grateful for my attention. Also, like so many women as they age, I put a higher value on a man's status in society, such as how successful he was, as well as how mature he is. So I guess all these things led me to be more attracted to that type. If I was to have dated a client, it would probably have been those that I looked to.

*   *   *

Were you ever confronted by the wives of clients? What happened?

I was never confronted. Some wives came in with their husbands for sessions, but I never had an irate wife tearing at my hair because her husband was visiting me. A couple of clients told me their wives found out about me because they found my phone number on a phone bill or in his phone book, and called to see what it was, but they never confronted me, just him.

*   *   *

Did the parents of doms who worked for you ever confront you? What happened?

I did meet a couple of mothers, single mothers, of girls who worked for me. They did not confront me. Their daughters took them to visit me. They were feminist or independent women and supported me in my legal battles, so there was no confrontation. To my knowledge very few of the girls who worked for me told their parents what they were up to, despite many of them appearing on the Internet or in trade paper ads undisguised.

*   *   *

Did you like torturing women?

Very much! They are prettier and more responsive and expressive than men. I liked torturing some women more than some men, but overall I like torturing men more.

*   *   *

What have your personal fantasies been over the years?

I have had and have several. One is being massaged with hot oil by several sexy men at once. I also have luxury fantasies such as shopping without looking at prices and being pampered in a beauty salon for hours. I would love to have a large house and order people about, but only if I felt like it at the time and not because they paid me to follow such a script. With all that being said, I would still role-play as a dominatrix from time to time, purely for the pleasure of it.

*   *   *

Did you prefer running the Bondage Bungalow in Thornhill or the Bondage Hotel and Sissy Maid Academy in Toronto?

I still can't say. The Thornhill house was serene and had beautiful grounds. It was so much less hectic than the Toronto house. There was also less financial pressure, with less overhead and fewer, if any employees. But the Toronto house was a major statement to society and figured in my legal battles and was a home for my daughter where we were finally reunited. I met so many more interesting people, both clients and others, at the Toronto house. Of course I was open there longer. So, I don't know. I would say that the Toronto house had more positives and negatives for me personally than did the Thornhill house, but today, looking back, I would say I appreciate them both equally.

*   *   *

Since you closed, have your former clients gone to other doms? How do you feel about that?

I have been in touch with several former clients who have visited other doms since, or doms who have mentioned them to me. I think that it's great that they do. After all, I couldn't see them any more even if I wanted to. The other doms are not competition to me any more.

*   *   *

Who was your favorite client of all time?

No comment, except to say it is not by a large margin that I would name one.

*   *   *

Did you ever lose control when torturing a helpless client? Were you ever tempted to go too far?

Never! For one thing, I was too scared of the possible consequences. For another, I had no reason to want to seriously hurt someone I had never met, or hardly met and who was paying me. I always respected the code words, meaning that if the client said to stop I did. However there were a few times when the guy was obviously a jerk and I thought he deserved more than I was dishing out, but I never lost control.

*   *   *

Do prostitutes want to be prostitutes?

Some do, some don't. Same with waitresses. Same with office cleaners. Same with factory workers. Same with nursing home orderlies. Women all over the place are doing things they might not wish to do, to earn a living. If a woman can make a living in a few hours a week, safely if the prostitution laws remain struck down, having sex rather than work many days a week in hard physical labor, shouldn't that be her choice?

*   *   *

Is sex work bad for society?

No, it's under-enforcement of laws against abuse of people, in all walks of life, that is bad for society. For example, weak enforcement of immigration laws in the workplace has led to sweatshops, illegal farm workers being exploited, illegal nannies, and illegal caregivers for the elderly, recruits for organized crime and so forth. Within each of those situations we see women being treated miserably and sexually abused. Why doesn't the government crack down on that? Why pick on the sex workers? It's a booming business. There is a market for the sale of sex and fantasy role play, not to mention hard core pornography, soft core pornography and "mommy porn". Almost everyone agrees these things are not going away and that people do not want to be told how to live their lives in private.

*   *   *

What are your views on feminism?

I was recently asked how I defined a feminist and whether I see myself as a feminist. I believe a feminist is a woman, or man for that matter, who believes in maximizing the equality of the sexes in every respect and minimizing discrimination of any type based on gender. I see myself as a feminist in terms of supporting equality of opportunity in the workplace, but I do not believe in pure equality in relationships. For example, as a dominatrix I see this desire of men to submit to women all the time, not to be equal. They want to revel in female superiority and worship a woman as a goddess, at least when they are role playing with them. I don't think that describes feminism in relationships.

*   *   *

Why is the image of the sex worker so often taboo?

This is a very difficult question to deal with for several reasons. For one thing, what does one mean by the term sex worker? Is a pure dominatrix a sex worker? Is a masseuse who does not tug as well as rub a sex worker? If a woman agrees to go on an expensive paid vacation with a man, but who is not directly paid, is she a sex worker? Is a stripper a sex worker? Is a porn actress a sex worker?

All that being said, let's just say that a sex worker is a man or woman who accepts money for the act of sexual intercourse. Even then, taboos of all types are very uneven. For example, in some circles in Europe being a mistress of an important man is considered prestigious for a woman.

So let's narrow it down further, and take the example of a woman in Canada who advertises in the paper as an escort and has sex with men in hotels for money, and is not being coerced by anyone. Let's look at the question of why anyone would object to that.

Well, for one thing, there are people who object to almost anything. Some condemn birth control. Some condemn pre-marital sex. Some condemn anonymous sex for free. Some people condemn cross-dressing. Some condemn homosexuality. Some condemn group sex. Some people condemn bondage and consensual and safe torture. Others condemn marriage. Some condemn having children in an overpopulated world.

I think that the reason the image of the sex worker is often taboo is because there are instances of young women being coerced or forced into the business by pimps. There is also some sentiment to the effect that women selling sex, even if it is fully voluntary and the women enjoys her work, is somehow immoral. There is some truth to the accusation that the sex worker makes it easier for one to cheat on their partner.

But as you know, sex work in Canada is not illegal and the laws restricting it were found unconstitutional. It is wrong to ban alcohol because some people drive drunk. It is wrong to ban sugar in food because some people are too fat. It is wrong to ban driving because some people are not careful. It is wrong to ban body contact sports because some athletes get hurt. Rather than ban the activities, such as drinking, society regulates them. But with sex, the idea of women being free and empowered is threatening to many male egos and women who have religious or other hang-ups.

CHAPTER 19

Final Words

I hope I have been able to give you a better idea of two worlds, so to speak.

One is that of the clients. Through their letters and what I advertised and taught my associates you can see what desires are out there. I think it's fair to say there are few men who in all honesty can say they are not or have never been interested in experiencing something I had to offer as a dominatrix. Those few may be happy with conventional love lives, or perhaps they like changing women often.

Then there are men like those whose letters you have been reading. In this book I listed many of the hundreds of things that could cause sexual arousal. I don't think there are many men, or women for that matter, who would not circle some items on that list of hundreds. I don't think there are many among us whose thoughts are not often a desire to do or be some of those things at times.

Diversity is becoming more tolerated and freedom more available. We know what the dangers of repression may be, but at the same time it brings up a very interesting question. What would happen if all men or women had the obstacles removed that prevented them from acting out their fantasies? What if all of them had the money and privacy to spend an evening each week doing what the authors of those letters and my other clients sought to do? What things should we continue to say no to? What is best left not discussed, even with one's dominatrix? What should we feel guilty about having done, or wanting to do? I don't know what the answers to these questions are.

What I do know is that the role play I engaged in with my clients was escapist recreation, but it was much more than that. It was an outlet for desires that occupied much of their daily thoughts. It had therapeutic value much of the time. The client was less repressed.

People are not the same person all the time. Men who were married and maybe had children told me they were not comfortable sharing these fantasies with their wives or girlfriends. They almost never had the equipment, facilities and privacy even in the unlikely event their wives were willing to engage in such role play. What would the children think? What if their wives left them and talked? How many wives would make a convincing dominatrix? Also, they had their roles as fathers, sons and members of the community to think of. Doing anything that might negatively impact on their reputation, fairly or unfairly, was not to be taken lightly. So they came to me.

Men see their wives and girlfriends in their everyday personas and appearances, and are familiar with them. That very familiarity, they say, destroys the illusion they might seek to create. It surprises me that any couples role play to begin with. I don't know whether to feel sorry for couples who role play or admire them. And let's not forget that some men and women are genuinely dominant and have a genuinely submissive partner and it is not role play—at least when they are in private (and maybe not even then). But, as I say, that would be a happy chance that rarely occurs in real life.

I am proud of making the dreams of these men come true. I am proud of often being their sole confidant. I am proud of helping men privately regress to childhood states or express their feminine personas, so they can symbolically revisit and address sublimated mild trauma from their early lives.

I am also glad I was able to give you a look into the other of the two worlds—mine. I am proud of my world.

Maybe now you can see why, when in leather and carrying a riding crop, fighting battles in court and so forth, I get so much attention in the media. I am speaking to human needs and wants that are denied to so many in their daily lives, but won't go away.

www.ingramcontent.com/pod-product-compliance
Lightning Source LLC
Chambersburg PA
CBHW030318290526
45785CB00001B/412